The McClure Collection

given by
J. WARREN and LOIS McCLURE

In support of the
RIT College of Business

Wallace Memorial Library
Rochester Institute of Technology

SUPER
SEARCHERS
COVER THE
WORLD

SUPER SEARCHERS COVER THE WORLD

The Online Secrets of
INTERNATIONAL BUSINESS RESEARCHERS

Mary Ellen Bates
Edited by Reva Basch

CyberAge Books

Information Today, Inc.
Medford, New Jersey

Super Searchers Cover the World:
The Online Secrets of International Business Researchers

Copyright © 2001 by Mary Ellen Bates

Super Searchers, Volume VIII
A series edited by Reva Basch

Liability

Trademarks

Library of Congress Cataloging-in-Publication Data

Bates, Mary Ellen.
    Super searchers cover the world : the online secrets of international business researchers / Mary Ellen Bates ; edited by Reva Basch.
        p. cm. – (Super searchers ; v. 8)
    Includes bibliographical references and index.
    ISBN 0-910965-54-4
        1. Business—Computer network resources. 2. Electronic information resource searching. I. Basch, Reva. II. Title. III. Series.

    HF54.56 .B38 2001
    025.06'65—dc21

                                                            2001047034

Printed and bound in the United States of America

Publisher: Thomas H. Hogan, Sr.
Editor-in-Chief: John B. Bryans
Managing Editor: Deborah Poulson
Copy Editor: Dorothy Pike
Proofreader: Susan Muaddi Darraj
Production Manager: M. Heide Dengler
Cover Designer: Jacqueline Walter
Book Designer: Kara Mia Jalkowski
Indexer: Enid Zafran

Dedication

In memory of my cousin, Peter Bates

About The Super Searchers Web Page

At the Information Today Web site, you will find *The Super Searchers Web Page*, featuring links to sites mentioned in this book. We will periodically update the page, removing dead links and adding additional sites that may be useful to readers.

The Super Searchers Web Page is being made available as a bonus to readers of *Super Searchers Cover the World* and other books in the Super Searchers series. To access the page, an Internet connection and Web browser are required. Go to:

www.infotoday.com/supersearchers

Table of Contents

Foreword

Today's business environment is expanding at a record pace as companies cross borders every day, building new offices in countries where, twenty years ago, most business executives would have thought they would never do business. The reality is that these countries have become the emerging markets for traditional business giants, and now even smaller companies are looking for less-saturated business arenas in which to market and sell their products and services.

This global expansion has created opportunity, but it has also placed a tremendous burden upon the shoulders of professional searchers who are asked to brief executives in their organizations about the ramifications of expansion—from geographical hindrances to competitive threats in the region. Many professional searchers began their careers as research librarians and moved on to become competitive intelligence specialists, market analysts, information specialists, or content managers. Now they are challenged to broaden their information horizons and expand across borders and oceans as their companies continue to grow and develop in emerging foreign markets.

Initially, searchers may have felt some trepidation when asked to produce in-depth research and analysis of markets, regional competitors, and demographics for countries or regions where their companies were planning to expand. Often the greatest challenge when searching for global information is not only relevance, but also finding the information in the language you need and seeing through the cultural nuances within that information. In addition, a thorough investigation of another country often involves extensive information-gathering efforts that are not a component of research easily found in your native country. This information may include foreign government regulations, culture, personnel issues, geography, and issues affecting the development of technical infrastructure.

It is important to keep in mind that a tremendous amount of knowledge exists within your own company, and the first step of a research project is to leverage the knowledge and experience of individuals within your own organization. In fact, the chances are in your favor that a large percentage of people within your organization have dealt with competitive, expansion, or partnership opportunities in regions all over the world. Today, networking within and outside of your organization to build relationships with people who are experienced in international business is more important than ever.

For example, if your company is evaluating an office expansion into Japan, first discuss this move with other offices in the Asia-Pacific region to understand how business and the local cultures work (or don't work) together in the region. This information will give you an understanding of the cultural issues that influence the region so that you can add the valuable, and often necessary, perspective to your final analysis and recommendations, giving decision makers a comprehensive picture of a region aside from the numbers and statistics pulled from market research. Furthermore, if you are lucky, your firm has, or is planning, a knowledge management strategy, which can save time and leverage the internal knowledge created through research and regular business operations.

Once you have the cultural understanding to apply unbiased perspective to the sources you find, you can begin the digging. This book provides valuable insight and practices to follow while searching for this information, but the greatest benefit of global business expansion and the Internet—the free and fee-based Internet—is that searching for this information is now much easier than it ever was. Before the advent of the Internet, finding the information you would need to provide a complete perspective of a country would have involved time in a library, possibly a trip to the country or region, and, often, significant time spent searching through outdated or inaccurate information.

The Internet brings to your fingertips thousands of sources—some more reliable than others—that can give you a detailed overview of a region, country, governments, culture, and other important issues. The key to effective searching on the Internet is discipline—building a structure into your searches, starting with the broad cultural overview and drilling deeper into the detail you need, as if you were searching based on the outline of the research report you are tasked to prepare. Starting research with a region rather than a country to understand the politics, cultures, and business environment will give you a thorough understanding of these issues and will start you on the trail to finding the remaining research to complete your report.

Another benefit of global business expansion is that online information services have been forced to acquire local content that is essential to the information-gathering process. The leaders of the information industry have realized this and built their content acquisition strategies around the premise that local information is becoming a precious commodity. These companies are acquiring the necessary content, and often translating it to meet the local language needs of professional searchers. In addition, industry leaders are building added functionality into their products with features including multilanguage user interfaces, the ability to search for content in specified languages, and XML capability that gives users the option to display information with a customized look and feel.

Super Searchers Cover the World examines the expert opinions and perspectives of professional searchers who have made indelible marks in their areas of expertise, effectively finding the information their organizations need to break the confines of their native markets and strategically expand their operations around the world. This book points out the importance of cultural awareness and gives you a strong understanding of how to find, evaluate, analyze, and present credible sources of global information. Good luck in your endeavors.

Clare Hart
President and CEO
Factiva, a Dow Jones and Reuters Company

Acknowledgments

Although I am listed as the author of *Super Searchers Cover the World*, the real authors of this book are the twenty Super Searchers I interviewed. I couldn't have written this one myself ... in fact, I learned something about global research from every interview. So, thank you, Arnoldo, Christine, Cris, Desmond, Federico, Geraldine, Kristin, Kyoko, Maribeth, Michele, Miranda, Peter, Rick, Ruth, Sheri, Teresa, Tracey, Valerie, Vicky, and Wes.

I am particularly grateful to all the Super Searchers whose first language is not English. I was so impressed by their willingness to spend an hour on the phone explaining complex research techniques and strategies, all in a second language. I cringe at the thought of my trying to do that in Spanish, the only other language with which I have a passing familiarity. I know how tiring it is, and I appreciate the graciousness of my interviewees as I asked them to spell out resources and repeat unfamiliar phrases.

I am also very grateful to Patty Shannon, transcriptionist extraordinaire. She listened to interviews with people speaking with a variety of accents, describing non-English sources, and on less-than-perfect telephone connections. As always, she did a superb job catching all the nuances and spelling out anything she didn't recognize. And when her husband and I found that we shared a passion for running marathons, her emailed transcripts would be accompanied with recommendations of upcoming marathons or commiseration on injuries. Talk about a full-service transcriptionist!

I would also like to thank Mary Mitchell of Factiva for all of the suggestions she sent me regarding people to interview. In addition, several of the Super Searchers themselves pointed me to other people with whom I simply *had* to talk. All of their referrals were great, and I very much appreciate how they expanded my global network.

I owe a great deal to Reva Basch, the editor of this book (and of the Super Searcher series), friend and colleague. My writing has improved immensely by my having worked with Reva over the years; by my count, this is the sixth book on which we've co-conspired, and I've enjoyed every one. And this is the third book that I have written for John Bryans of Information Today. He is a delightful person to work with and an excellent dinner companion, although it seems that most of those dinners have resulted in my promising to write another book.

And finally, I want to thank Alex Kramer—friend, fellow entrepreneur, and running partner—who is responsible for getting me out of the office and on the running path on a regular basis; and Dave and Lucy, my household muses.

Introduction

OK, I'll admit it. I was an online searcher back when online wasn't yet cool. We had 300-baud modems with acoustic couplers, and the results of our research were printed on thermal paper that curled up and faded within a few weeks. Those of us in the U.S. never thought to "limit" our research to U.S. sources; we rarely found any citations to articles published elsewhere.

The first shock to us old-time searchers was the advent of full-text sources online. The possibilities seemed endless; we could actually print out an entire article without having to send someone to the local library with a fistful of dimes for the photocopier. We thought that we had finally reached the peak of online research capabilities—we had (fee-based) access to both the full text of English-language material and citations to materials in other languages.

Then came the Web. All of a sudden, being able to download yesterday's newspaper article was not that cool anymore. What was perhaps most disconcerting from the perspective of an online researcher was the fact that entirely new kinds of information were becoming available. Governments were making reports and statistics available that had never before seen the light of day. Associations were using the Web to promote the interests of their members. Companies were loading technical product specifications, executives' biographies, financial information and—of course—sales literature on their Web pages. Advocacy groups were able to disseminate to the world information on their points of view. Not only was information available on the Web that had never been digitized before, but organizations were publishing information on the Web that they had never thought of even developing before. When the cost of publication is virtually nil and the

1

barrier to entry is as low as the cost of a Web site, it seems that everyone with a point of view can publish it, and does.

Online researchers have reacted to the Web with both enthusiasm and skepticism. The ability to tap into all these new information sources is a wonderful thing; it enables us to answer questions that we could never handle before. On the other hand, many researchers look at the Web much as a gardener looks at a field of wildflowers. You know there is a lot of great material there, but there are also plenty of weeds, exotics, and nasty pests. The challenge is to find the useful and unique resources while avoiding the ticks, brambles, and poison ivy.

One of the unexpected effects of the Web has been to raise the awareness about the information sources that lie beyond one's own borders. Type the word "astronomy" in a search engine, for example, and you are likely to find Web sites from all over the world, and from groups as varied as the U.S. government-funded NASA, Bonn University, an amateur astronomer's personal home page, the Canada-France-Hawaii Telescope Corporation, and the U.K.'s Particle Physics and Astronomy Research Council—and those are just a few of the English-language sites! A casual Web surfer could be excused for thinking that, with such variety, *everything* must be on the Web.

However, many researchers also know that the Web is, in many ways, a kilometer wide and a centimeter deep. While the national governments of most countries have established Web sites, for instance, many of them contain very little information and virtually no in-depth reports or research. Publicly traded companies in some countries, such as the U.S., are required to make available detailed financial statements and information on the markets in which they compete. Companies in countries that do not have such strict disclosure laws may provide far less information on their Web sites. This means that researchers often find that the expectations of their clients, especially regarding the range and depth of information available on the Web, far exceed reality.

Looking Beyond Borders

This is the first book I have written as a direct result of audience reaction to presentations I have given at information conferences. After I finished *Super Searchers Do Business* [Information Today, Inc., 1999], I gave a number of talks about research tips from the Super Searchers. Every time, without fail, I would get at least one question from the audience along the lines of, "This is very useful, but how do we find the equivalent information in Latin America, or Asia, or Europe?" The night after one of these presentations, at Internet Librarian International in London, I went out to dinner with John Bryans, head of the book publishing division at Information Today. I am not quite clear how this happened, but by the end of the evening, I found that I had agreed to do a book on global Super Searchers.

I took a deep breath and started thinking of all the people I knew, or had heard about, who were experienced, excellent international researchers proficient in finding information using a wide variety of resources. Unfortunately, I had to limit my search to those who speak English; I speak a little Spanish but not enough to carry on a conversation and certainly not enough to conduct an interview. My greatest challenge, though, proved to be narrowing down the list of possible interviewees; there are so many Super Searchers who understand the nuances of finding information not only within their own countries or regions, but around the world.

This book contains fifteen interviews with a total of twenty people from North America, Latin America, Europe, and Asia. I only wish I had been able to include *all* the people to whom I was referred while working on this book. In the pages that follow, you will hear from librarians and information center managers who provide research services throughout their organizations; independent information professionals who offer research services to clients around the world; information professionals who acquire, manage, and develop information products within their organizations; and two Super Searchers who work in academic settings and whose jobs include teaching students how to conduct global research.

From my interviews with all these global Super Searchers, I gained a greater appreciation for the challenges of searching outside the borders of one's own country or region. So much of *my* research has focused on North America and western Europe, and I realize what a charmed life I live, informationally speaking. The U.S. government has enough money to count everything, it seems, and to make the information available on the Web. A significant portion of English-language newspapers, magazines, trade newsletters, and journals are available online, either on the Web or on the professional online services. Telephone research in the U.S., while never easy, is at least feasible; the people we call are usually no more than three time zones away, and they invariably speak English. What I did find somewhat heartening was the confirmation that global research is just plain hard. It's not just me. Expanding research to cover a number of countries or regions exponentially increases the complexity and difficulty of the information gathering.

"It's Not What You Know, It's Who Will Talk to You"

As Super Searcher Miranda van Roosmalen commented, sometimes we have to look for people, not information. That is, our first step is often to find a person who can point us in the right direction, who knows the essential information sources, or who has access to the full text of documents that do not exist electronically. Many of the searchers in this book had similar comments. One question that I asked during each of the interviews was about the most frustrating or difficult part of global research. Many people mentioned the lack of local sources, in their local language, in electronic format. Yes, they could find articles from U.S. sources online, but they need electronic access to their own country's newspapers, magazines, and academic journals. What often happens is that researchers are limited to hard-copy sources they keep in-house, or to the information they can find from asking local experts.

Another interesting comment I heard several times was that no one person can really do *global* research. Each country and region of the world has its own quirky resources, its own information culture, and its own laws and customs—both written and unwritten—regarding disclosure of information. Sometimes, it's a matter of knowing the information landscape, having that gut sense that what you have found so far is probably 90 percent of what is out there. Super searchers become adept at figuring out the lay of the land and finding basic information, then working their contacts to find an in-country expert who can help dig up all the resources that are visible only to someone on the ground.

Looking for Information in the *Least* Likely Sources

Several Super Searchers mentioned the need to look beyond what have become the traditional sources—print reference materials, CD-ROM databases, the professional online services, and what can be found via Web search engines—to new sources, including information that resides only in the heads of local experts. In addition, global research often involves finding the "gray literature" from international organizations—the tremendously valuable reports, white papers, and other documents not actively promoted or listed in standard publication catalogs. Knowing where to look for gray literature is the challenge; many international organizations make their reports and statistics available on Web sites, but the material may be buried beyond the reach of search engines.

I also heard a number of comments about gathering *consistent* information across borders. With the notable exception of the European Union, it is hard to find comparable numbers when looking at statistics from several countries. Data-gathering techniques differ; time series differ; timeliness of data differs; even definitions of what is being counted differ. This makes it virtually impossible for researchers to develop templates or guides to information sources, as very few resources span the globe. Instead of working from a familiar checklist of the usual, reliable sources, global researchers must often create a new checklist with each project.

Another of my interview questions was about cultural blind spots—those situations in which a research question simply makes no sense when translated from one culture to another, or when the client assumes that information about one country will be disclosed or made accessible simply because it is available in another country. As much as we all try to be culturally sensitive, this continues to be a problem. One of the underappreciated skills of a good researcher is the ability to help a client rework a research project to appropriately reflect the economic and cultural climate of the region being researched, and to take into account the different information sources available.

Globalising My Spell-Checker

I need to explain the spelling and grammar in this book. In fact, as I ran the initial chapters through a word-processing spell-checker, an interesting question came up that neither Reva nor I had thought of before: What version of English should we use in each chapter? The portions of this book that I wrote—the Acknowledgments, Introduction, and Appendix—use American English spelling. For the Super Searchers whose native language is English, I used the spelling of their country. So the interviews with Maribeth Bacig, Wes Edens, Sheri Lanza, Michele Marinak, Ruth Pagell, Rick Reynen, Peter Sidney, and Christine Windheuser are in American English. The interviews with Geraldine Clement-Stoneham, Tracey Collinson, Vicky Connor, Desmond Crone, Cris Kinghorn, Kristin Michie, and Teresa St. Clair are in the Queen's English. For the Super Searchers whose first language is not English, I defaulted to the spelling of English that they would use: American English for Valerie Matarese, Arnoldo Sterinzon, and Federico Turnbull; and British English for Miranda van Roosmalen. Kyoko Toyoda's interview was conducted via email, so I retained her (American English) spelling throughout.

A curious result of this exercise in bilingual English was that I now find myself inadvertently adopting the British spelling of words such as *behaviour*, *organisation*, and *labour*. And I have learned (or learnt) to run any email that I am sending to a British colleague through a mental U.K.-English spell-checker.

One other housekeeping note is in order. Within each chapter, the first mention of each information resource carries a number referring to its listing in the Appendix. I have written the annotations in the Appendix, and any errors in description are mine, not the interviewees'. I have attempted to include current cost information if a resource is fee-based, and I have listed the cost in the local currency. While these descriptions are current as of mid-2001, it is inevitable that some sites will have changed by the time you read this book. A current listing of these URLs is available at www.infotoday.com/ supersearchers.

Finally, I want to acknowledge again my gratitude to all the people who so generously gave their time and shared their expertise in this book. I learned something from each interview, and I trust that you, too, will find the insights of these global Super Searchers valuable.

Ruth Pagell
International Business Educator

Ruth Pagell is the Executive Director of the Goizueta Business Library at Emory University, in Atlanta, Georgia.

rpagell@emory.edu
www.emory.edu/LIB/CBI

Can you tell me a little bit about your background, how you got where you are today, and how much of your work involves international research?

I've been a librarian for a long time, and I've been a business librarian for about twenty years now. I started out as a business librarian at Drexel University, and I then moved up to become Associate Director at the Lippincott Library of the Wharton School at the University of Pennsylvania. In 1994, I came to my current position at Emory to start up a business library. It sounded like fun, which was the reason I took the job.

But what really got me interested in international research was the opportunity in 1989 to be an American Library Association/U.S. Information Agency fellow in Bangkok, Thailand, at the Asian Institute of Technology. I was there for a year, and when I came back, in addition to the writing and speaking about business information that I had been doing before, I was asked to start speaking about international business information. That meant

7

that I started really having to *do* research on international business information. There's nothing like being asked to speak about a topic to get you up to speed!

When I gave my first big talk on international business resources at an American Library Association conference, several people asked me to write a book about international research. I batted the idea around and didn't really want to do it. But my boss, Mike Halperin, and I were talking about it and finally he said, "Oh, let's do a book." So we wrote *International Business Information: How to Find It, How to Use It* [184, see Appendix]. We have done two editions, but we don't plan on updating it again; it just doesn't make sense anymore to do a print book in an area that is changing so rapidly. When we did the first edition, we spent months scouring the world to find enough sources to put in the book, because nothing was out there. By the time we did the second edition, the challenge was trying to find *quality* information.

How many of the library's patrons are from outside the U.S.?

A third of the graduate student body at the Goizueta Business School is international. Their perspective in terms of what information they expect to be available is very different from that of the U.S. students. All of our students have to take an international course called "Global Perspectives," which is the most research-intensive course that they take in the business school. As part of the course, they have to do a large research assignment. That means that they spend a lot of time with the librarians. While they don't have to live in the library, because so much of our information is distributed online, they still spend an awful lot of time with the librarians.

Can you describe a typical project that the students in the Global Perspectives course would tackle?

I have a couple of examples. One of them is fairly typical; they're supposed to be looking at an industry. Many choose to study the telecommunications industry, because a lot of our students come from telecommunications firms, although we've also had people do topics as varied as shipbuilding and cigars. Cigars was one of the more interesting ones.

Whatever industry they choose, the students are supposed to be looking at three countries, so they usually choose the U.S., Japan or a country in Europe, and a developing country, and they try to see the prospects for their selected industry in those countries.

When they come to the library, are the students looking for training in how to use the library's resources, or do they need help with actually finding the information? What's the librarian's role in all of this?

I'm glad you asked that question, because we pride ourselves on our role in this course in particular. We work very closely with the faculty member. We first go into the class and show them a Web page that we have created for them, where they can start. We say to them, "Go through this checklist on the Web, and if you can't find anything about your industry, you're going to have problems with this assignment." The Web page is at www.emory.edu/LIB/CBI/intpersp.htm, and it's available to the public.

Then we tell the students that we will set up special training sessions for the databases they have not encountered in the research they've done up until now. For example, the class I am working with this semester is composed of executives, and they have some background and training in competitive strategy. But they haven't seen things like ISI [78] or Global Market Information Database [56] or EIU [37], so they need training on those products. With a class of executives, we will train whoever comes; sometimes it is hard to get them to come in for training. When it's a class of MBA students, we suggest they send one person from each group, to keep us from being inundated with too many students at once.

The other thing that we do, while they're in the initial stages of deciding what their research topic will be, is to recommend strongly that they make an appointment with somebody on the library staff, and that staff person has often become part of the group. Most semesters, we see three-quarters of the groups at least twice. We tell the students that we'll bat around some project ideas with them—we really make a point of telling them how much we will work with them. We listen to them, hear them talk about their projects, tell them some of the pros and cons from an Internet information perspective of what they're working on. Of course, some of them have gone ahead and worked on a project after we told them that we wouldn't recommend it.

What kind of research project isn't as good from a research perspective?

Some of the newer industries, unfortunately. It's very hard to find the kind of data they need when they're doing projects concerning e-commerce, for example. When they try to get trade statistics on service industries, they have to realize that the data's just not there; it's not being collected for service industries. Some projects are difficult because, while they are supposed to focus on the industry level, the students will select a product that makes up far too little of an industry. In those cases, we might tell them that they're going to have trouble finding the kind of macro information that's needed for this kind of assignment.

Sometimes the issue is their choice of countries. Europe is fine, but some regions are tough to research. It's really hard to do research on Africa, for example. We do the best we can; we get whatever data we can get out of the traditional governmental organizations and whatever we can pull out of EIU. A couple of projects last semester included Africa; one project had to do with healthcare and one with education. That wasn't too bad, because the UN [139] had data on it. The students really enjoyed doing research that wasn't as business-oriented as usual. They said, "You know, we have lots of opportunities to do business stuff. In this class we can expand our horizons and our research a bit." They enjoyed going farther afield and looking at some environmental issues.

What changes over the past few years have you seen in the availability of electronic resources covering the international arena?

Obviously, international coverage is much greater. When we were working on the first edition of our book, it was just dreadful; it was really hard to find things. Resources like World Reporter [155] or Reuters Business Briefing [115] or the multilingual newspapers in LexisNexis [88] or Dow Jones Interactive [35] are certainly a big improvement. ISI, despite some of its problems, is a great addition. Global Market Information Database is a wonderful timesaver for my staff and students, because things are compiled in one place.

From the perspective of the free Web, one of the huge challenges has always been finding information, particularly financial or economic data, for individual countries; there was no way you were going to get subscriptions to the statistical office's publications or the central bank's publications. In any sizable library, the serials department would kill you if you tried to claim all the issues or items that didn't come in. Now, so much of this information is available on the Web.

It's great; you can get the local news on the Web. When we do these Global Perspectives courses, we keep telling the students that they should be looking at global sources first, not U.S. sources, to see what's being said. We have access to all kinds of international newspapers on a daily basis, whereas before the Web, we just had compilations. There are some real problems with that, but at least the material is out there. There's so much more information and, particularly for material from outside the

U.S., the information is really good and very useful for researchers.

Are you finding that most countries have their basic statistical information on the Web now?

Yes and no. Most countries have a link to their central bank or their national statistical office. But what you find when you get there varies a lot. The Bank of Poland and Bank of Slovenia, for example, have really good data. Thailand does a good job with their data. But sometimes all you get is a message to "buy this," and you don't know ahead of time the quality of what you are buying.

What is really raising the quality of the fiscal data for countries is the effort of the IMF (International Monetary Fund) [75] to standardize data through the Special Data Dissemination Standard and the General Data Dissemination System. Now, we are seeing more consistency among countries in how they report financial data. About a year ago, something like twenty countries had signed on, saying that they were going to abide by the IMF's standards. Six months later, fifteen more countries had signed on. And of course, from a financial perspective, all of the ADRs are putting a lot of pressure on companies in other countries.

ADRs?

American Depository Receipts, which are publicly traded stocks that represent a specific number of shares in a non-U.S. stock. This makes it a lot easier for U.S. investors to purchase shares of a non-U.S. company, since they avoid currency exchange issues. But with all this investment in non-U.S. companies, U.S. investors are demanding a higher level of company information than was available before. So this information is becoming much more readily available, for both investors and researchers.

Of course, it still depends on the company and on the country where it's headquartered. German companies used to be very reluctant to disclose financial information. They weren't trading on the U.S. exchanges because they just didn't want to give out this information. They have been slow to come on board, but more and more of this information is becoming available.

Do you have any problem judging the quality of the information? Has it gotten more difficult with the increased availability of information on the Web?

It's never been easy, but certainly it's more difficult now, because we don't know some of the people who are putting information out there. At least in the U.S., it's fairly easy to find out more about an information source. But I'll see something that was put out in, say, an Eastern European country, and I have no way of knowing if this person is a valid information provider or just somebody selling an ISP [Internet service provider] site, which is often the case. You can look at Web-based company directories and find out that they actually include only those companies that happen to have their Web site hosted by a particular ISP.

We try to use standard evaluation tools. For example, I always look for a topic that I know something about, to see if the answer makes sense. And if the answer doesn't make sense on the first topic I try, maybe this isn't fair, but I assume that it may not be reliable for topics I *don't* know much about.

I also look at dates, of course, to see when the site has been updated, because obviously that's important. Someone may have put up a lot of international material because they thought it was a good idea at one point, but they have never come back to revise it. If the site says "contact us," I often do email them to see whether they respond and if they even understand my question. On the other hand, I maintain a Web site with about 500 links on it, and unfortunately I haven't looked at the links in two months. I know that I have some dead links in there, too.

What is the biggest challenge you run into when you're doing global research?

The biggest problem is comparability. Countries report statistics in different units, and there are different amounts of information available from one country to another. If a researcher is just focusing on one country, it's not that much of a problem. But when you're doing research across countries, then it becomes a really big problem in terms of consistency and comparability.

Another problem is finding information about nontraditional industries. Not that it's simple in the U.S., but it certainly is much more difficult internationally. There is no census of service industries for the world.

Getting a handle on everything is a huge problem. It's hard to just stay on top of the resources that are available. If I see an interesting resource that isn't relevant to what I am working on right now, I won't remember it. When I do need it, I just have to go back and do the research again, and see what I can find.

If my staff members know what a student's topic is, they generally will do some research up front, before the student's appointment, to scan the information environment and see what is out there. That helps them ask better questions during the appointment, because they have a sense of what's available. I'm always concerned when somebody ends up having to meet with me instead of one of my staff members, because I just don't have the time to do that preliminary research. Luckily, the rest of the staff do have the time to do this preparation, and that enables them to provide better service to the students.

What do you do when the only sources that you need are in a language that you don't speak?

We can't handle the interpretation of non-English-language sources, but we have so many international students that, in many cases, somebody speaks the language that's needed. This is where it's easier dealing with international students than with business people. The students usually select the countries they are going to study based on who is in the group. If they are look-ing at Brazil, one of the group members undoubtedly speaks Portuguese. They're going to have somebody who speaks Chinese if they are researching China, or somebody who speaks Russian if they are researching Russia. So all we have to do is get them to sites that have the information they need, even if they are foreign-language sites, and they can take it from there. A lot of the students are sophisticated enough to be aware of some of the basic business sites from their own countries. If I were deal-ing with a business person, I don't know what I would do. AltaVista's Babelfish [201] translation isn't going to do it.

What about cultural blind spots, particularly when the students are conducting research on a country they're not familiar with?

Yes, although it is less of a problem when someone from that country is in their group. A lot of our blind spots have to do with understanding cultural differences, and what those cultural dif-ferences mean. In some countries, the information you're going to find is just not going to be at the level you were expecting; it won't reveal what you might have thought it would include. Some cultures don't tend to disclose as much, or they will report information in a masked way. There are lots of horror stories about people doing market research who didn't understand these differences and got results that made absolutely no sense, because they didn't know the culture of the country. The ques-tions they asked were not the same as the questions "heard" by the person being interviewed. And they were asking the ques-tions of the wrong people.

What other challenges do you run into when doing global research?

We have a hard time getting demographic data—not informa-tion like how many people live in a particular city, but lifestyle data. People think, well, you can get ZIP code data for the U.S., so why can't you get it for the rest of the world? The kinds of questions we ask about demographics are so cultural; sometimes the question itself is irrelevant outside the U.S. The whole idea of how you categorize a population really depends on having certain assumptions about how the population divides itself up. That could be considered another cultural blind spot; people use U.S. terminology for countries that didn't go through the same population or economic cycles.

Another challenge is that people want city data at a much more detailed level than we can get for them. In some cases, the information exists and we just can't get it; in some cases, it doesn't exist anywhere. It's tempting sometimes to refer students to the market research firms that have this information. But one of the problems with dealing with students is that you don't want students with money to have an advantage over students who can't afford to purchase market research. So it becomes very tricky if resources are available that you would have to pay for. We do try to steer them to associations or government agencies as possible sources. When it's a faculty member asking the question, then we give them names of fee-based resources that they could purchase out of their research budget.

How do you know when to stop doing research, especially when you are doing research for faculty members?

It depends on what they need, what they're expecting from us, and how much they will do themselves. It's the same thing with domestic research, really. In our case, because it's all pro bono, part of the equation is how much time you can spend on this project. That isn't a good measure of when to stop, but it is what we must use. We will try everything we know. We talk to each other, we talk to other people in the university, but if nothing else is available, then we say, "This is what we've been able to do. Let us know if this is okay." If it's not okay—if they want more information—often all we can do is give them names of additional people to contact.

I use a continuum for gauging whether I have probably found most of the available information. It's based on the country I am researching, the company or industry, the size of the geographic area. I'm sure it's not completely accurate in all cases, but at least it gives me an idea of what to expect. For example, I was preparing for some teaching in Poland, and I decided to research a Polish computer company as an example. It was publicly traded, so when I didn't turn up anything in the places where I thought I would find information, I assumed that the sources weren't covering it well and I needed to look a whole lot harder. I felt that the information had to be there and I should be able to find it, since I knew the country in which the company was located, and I knew that it was publicly traded. If it had been a publicly traded computer company in Nigeria, I probably wouldn't have looked as hard.

It sounds like a lot of it is just common sense and experience in knowing that there should be more information out there.

Right. I know the European Union has a lot of rules about what can and can't be made public. I know that countries that want to join the EU are working really hard to make as much information available as possible, so sometimes I would expect more from an EU-wannabe country than from other countries.

And of course, we use both commercial sites and Web sites for most of our research. I think we're at a time when we need to be using both. We're certainly not going to find all the information we need free on the Web, and we're certainly not going to find it all in our commercial sources, either. A thorough search requires both types of research.

Speaking of Web research, do you rely on country-specific search engines? Where do

you start when you're doing global research on the Web?

Search engines in general are not the first place I go for most things. I would be more likely to go to a topic-specific mega-site. Or I'll start with a government agency and see if it provides any relevant links. When I've used a country-specific search engine, I have found that the quality has been really iffy. That might have been the countries I chose, I don't know. When I am doing international research, I would rather go directly to a site I know, or to a portal or a mega-site.

What sources on the open or free Web do you consider essential for global research?

The World Bank [153], the International Trade Administration [146], FedStats [49], and the U.S. State Department [145], where you can get the Country Commercial Guides. And, as I mentioned, I rely on mega-sites to link to central banks, national statistics offices, chambers of commerce, embassies, and stock exchanges. My staff has built a Web page called "Key International Resources," [82] with most of the resources that we recommend. My staff hates the page because it's not pretty, but it has links to all the resources we rely on, including the mega-sites I use the most. We have a link to the University of Michigan's International Business Resources on the WWW [73], for example.

My only worry is whether the people who build and maintain these mega-sites put in the same amount of time that I do, and have the same kind of knowledge and ability to evaluate what they are putting on their sites. I have a friend who says, "Well, if it's an academic institution, then it should be good," and my response is, "But a lot of academic institutions have not been providing the level of international research that we have, and I wonder if the material is all that reliable." If it's free, then it's going to look good to some people, but they may not really know what the material is or how good it is. I also use some of the company directory sites, such as Kompass [83], even though it's not entirely free, or Europages [43], for people who need to get started with company lists.

And what fee-based services are must-haves?

Until last month it was Stat-USA [127], but that is being decimated. They haven't updated information in the National Trade Data Bank in years. And now you cannot get the U.S. Merchandise Trade data from Stat-USA; you have to have a separate subscription to USA Trade Online [150]. Now they are distributing the market reports and country commercial guides elsewhere for free, so you don't have to go to Stat-USA and pay to get them, although the search engines are usually terrible elsewhere.

So, while Stat-USA used to be our first choice, it's not anymore. Now we're using ISI and Dow Jones Interactive. We have to change DJI's default set of publications searched, from the usual collection of major news and business sources to a more global selection of publications. It's tough to get users to remember to change the publications-searched field. And we use LexisNexis Universe, although it's difficult to get to their World Library. As I mentioned earlier, we use the Global Market Information Database and EIU for much of our research as well.

Of course, which source we use depends on the question. We couldn't manage without Global Access [54]. It provides access to international companies, and much of the information is just not readily available elsewhere, particularly the financials in the format in which we need them.

How do you hear about new online resources, particularly ones that don't get a lot of publicity in the U.S.?

I used to do a much better job of it, because as long as I was working on the book, I would always attend the Online Information conference [212] held in London every year. I found that one to be the best conference, the best source for international information resources. However, I haven't gone in a couple of years. Now I just do a lot of research on my own to try to figure out what's out there. It's difficult, because a lot of resources aren't of very good quality.

How do you think international research has changed over the past few years?

There has been a very gradual change in the mindset of business researchers, from U.S.-focused to more internationally focused. Because business is so global, it's hard to think solely within a country's borders. I see more of a trend toward looking at questions in a global way, not just thinking in terms of what's available in U.S. sources. You have to ask, "Okay, what am I going to find for this, worldwide?" I am even seeing differences in how people are framing their questions. The globalization in the information industry will have some impact on consistency, and will enable us to compare data across countries. Most of our major information vendors are not U.S. companies any more.

I think more non-English content will become available. There is probably a lot of content in non-English languages that we don't see, that we never find, because we're searching in English to begin with. That is another of those blind spots; we are still thinking of the concepts in English. With the globalization of business, there's going to be more non-English information out there. There's probably going to be more junk as well as more quality information. We're also finding much more *demand* for data, particularly from non-U.S. sources.

What other advice would you give someone who is tackling international research?

First, accuracy is relative. I got that idea from an interview with Gary Mueller, who was the president of Internet Securities ["Internet Securities: An Emerging Service for an Emerging Niche Market" *Database*, October 1997, page 56]. As much as we want quality, we cannot expect the same standards from emerging markets as from U.S. sources. We have to remember that the information we find may not be what we might hope for, but it's better than nothing.

Another thing I tell businesspeople in particular is that if it's free on the Web, it might not have any comparative advantage. And just because you can find it for the U.S. doesn't mean you're going to find it for the rest of the world. In terms of doing quality global research, it's really important to take some time to learn about international business, to understand the EU and EU directives, to learn a little bit about international accounting, and to look into international trade. I try not to take anything from an unvetted Web site, a site I've never seen before. If it looks odd, I try to double-check it someplace else. I send questions or comments to Web site owners to see if they're going to get back to me. If I'm working with owners of small businesses, I always recommend that they either go to a local chamber of commerce or the U.S. Department of Commerce's Commercial Service [143] in the country they are researching.

Super Searcher Power Tips

➤ When I'm evaluating an information resource, I always look for a topic that I know something about, to see if the answer makes sense. If it doesn't, I assume that it may not be reliable for topics I don't know much about.

➤ The questions we ask about demographics are so cultural; sometimes the question itself is irrelevant outside the U.S. How you categorize a population depends on having certain assumptions about how the population divides itself up.

➤ There is a lot of content out there in non-English languages, which we don't see because we're searching
in English to begin with.

➤ From the perspective of the free Web, one of the huge
challenges has always been finding information, particularly financial or economic data, for individual
countries.

➤ When I am doing international research, I prefer to go
directly to a site I know, or to a portal or a mega-site.

➤ We're certainly not going to find all the information
we need free on the Web, and we're certainly not
going to find it all in our commercial sources, either. A
thorough search requires both types of research.

Federico Turnbull

Mexico-Based Researcher and Online Trainer

Federico Turnbull is Director of AEID, SC, in Mexico City, Mexico. AEID offers access to professional information through online searching and document delivery services. The company specializes in Mexican and Latin American information sources and provides training in the use of electronic information and the Internet.

aeid@solar.sar.net

First, why don't you tell me a little bit about your background and how you started your business?

I have a bachelor's degree in chemical engineering from the University of Veracruz in Mexico, and a master's degree in science information from the Illinois Institute of Technology. I worked at the National University of Mexico until 1986, when I became independent. I was working at the National Information Center for the Sciences and Humanities at the university, and I was in charge of the Science Information Division, so I was doing a lot of online searching. Then I saw that I had the potential of starting a business, and that's what I did. Actually, I had started my own business in 1982, but I really went independent in 1986. What drove me to do that was that I became a representative of

23

Dialog Information Services [33, see Appendix] for Mexico, and then the rest of Latin America, and that lasted from 1986 to 1994.

I had my information brokerage business, but I was mostly devoted to dealing with issues related to Dialog, like customer support and training and things like that, so I didn't do much work for my own clients. When I ended my job representing Dialog, I continued working for them in 1995 as an external consultant. At that time, Knight-Ridder bought Dialog and opened offices in several parts of the world, including Mexico. They decided to open a local office, since they wanted to be officially represented by Dialog employees rather than by an outside contractor. However, I decided to continue with my own business as well. I had a lot of experience in online searching, mostly with the Dialog system, of course, and I did quite a bit of searching for clients. In 1996, I decided to go to work for an Internet service provider, because I saw that I had to learn the Internet business. It was a very good experience; I learned how to relate to telecommunications people, how the Internet worked as a network, and the jargon of the industry.

Then I went back to my business full time in 1997. It's had its ups and downs, with my going in and out of full-time employment, but I never really left online searching and training and selling information products. Now, my company does training on the use of electronic information sources. I have several years of experience in teaching Dialog, but now it's more balanced because I don't have to teach one system in particular. I present everything that is available, mostly in the areas of business and industry, since that's where I work most. I also do online searching, mostly using the fee-based online services, and some document delivery work.

Most of my clients are from Mexico, but now I have some clients from abroad, thanks to referrals from the Association of Independent Information Professionals [208]. AIIP has helped a lot; I've been working with several colleagues from AIIP. I still do some work representing vendors as well. About 60 percent of my clients are based here in Mexico, about 25 percent are based in other Latin American countries, and the remaining 15 percent are mostly from the United States, Canada, and Europe.

What has made life so interesting is that I have managed to get a pretty complete picture of the online searching environment. First I was in the scientific academic environment; then I worked in the humanities department of the National University; then I went independent and focused on business research.

My business is growing fast because, with NAFTA and commercial trade agreements with the European Union, more and more people from abroad are looking for Mexican information and for people who can provide research services. Of course, both my Mexican and my foreign clients need international research. With the explosion of information on the Internet, we have a lot of local sources now, but for years we had to rely only on international sources such as Dialog, LexisNexis [88], and the other online systems to get external information. Our clients still require that kind of information, of course. It is interesting; when the Internet first became popular, the demand for information research dropped. But there has been a backlash, as clients have discovered that they cannot easily find the information on the Internet by themselves. Now they realize that, first, it isn't that fast, and second, they don't have any criteria to decide whether what they find is of quality or not. So they are using us again; the demand for professional research is growing again. At this point, I would say that we fill about 50 percent of the information requests from international sources and the other 50 percent from local sources.

Could you describe a typical international research project?

Sometimes clients just need information from the U.S. or Canada, or from North America generally. Sometimes it's the whole of the Americas, or Europe, and, to a lesser extent, all of the world. Most of these international searches deal with markets, companies, or products on which we have to find information. For example, we do a lot of research on foreign trade, identifying suppliers and distributors. Clients usually need to know what companies are involved in which countries, what they do, what they import or export, how much foreign trade they do, and things like that.

If we can find a reliable international information source that encompasses several countries, then we use that first. Sometimes we have to do the research country by country; that's what happens most often when we are researching Latin American companies. Most of the Latin American countries are beginning to put their information online, and, fortunately, more and more reliable information is available online. But there hasn't been much integration among the sources, so it's very hard to find a full Latin American database. We have to go country by country, and we find that the quality varies from source to source, and some sources are more detailed than others. Fortunately, it looks like vendors are dealing with these issues; they are realizing that integration of information and consistency of the data is very important.

For research that compares countries in Europe or North America, or the entire world, we use more global information sources. We often use Kompass [83] and Dun & Bradstreet [36]. For Latin American research, we mostly use government information; we don't have very many local business products yet, except in Mexico. The problem with relying on government information is that it can be biased, but that's all we have. We just have to use our judgment on how reliable and how current the information is.

And, you know, when I ask colleagues for suggestions on other information sources, it turns out that the ones they recommend are not really online—they are mostly CD-ROM or printed sources. We still use a lot of CD-ROMs here in Latin America.

One thing that I've learned over the years is that it's very important to know how exhaustive or specific you should be in your research. If you have to be exhaustive, then you not only have to use the general information sources, but you also have to go to the specific sources for each country. In that case, you have to take into account the cultural issues and unspoken assumptions about information—what is available, and what is not available. It's not like a simple search on Dialog, where you can do a single search of all of the relevant databases and see what comes up.

It's very, very important to know the sources, and the reliability of the sources. That's one question that people always ask me when I am doing training: "How can we know if a source that we find on the Web is reliable or not?" Part of it is knowing the information source, knowing if it is a reliable company that compiles reliable information. That's why some information sources cost money, because they can assure you that the information is reliable. I recommend that they take into account the reliability of the local sources, how they work, and the cultural differences in each country. There is a saying that Latin America is a group of countries separated by the same language. You might think that Mexico is similar to Argentina or Colombia, but there are significant cultural differences.

What changes have you seen in international information resources over the last few years?

Oh, the Internet has made a big difference in how we do research. It has been a real blessing. It was so hard to get Latin American information before the Internet. We could only use traditional online systems to get Latin American information, or we would have to write to or visit government offices, and that takes a lot of time. Thanks to the Internet, more and more local information is readily available. It's interesting; on the one hand, you have educational institutions that have put all their content online—their publications, their libraries, their documents. On the other hand, you have government offices that are including more and more information on their Web sites. I think they still have a long way to go, compared to the U.S., where you have lots of government documents and information sources online. Here you only have the most important ones. But, it's a beginning; it's a start.

The information companies here still see e-business as primarily selling through online catalogs. Very few have true e-commerce yet. So they show you a catalog of their products on the Web, but then you have to buy the product in the traditional way, by calling them or mailing or faxing an order.

What is the biggest challenge that you run into when you're doing international research?

The biggest challenge is that Latin American information is just not available online, or not readily available online, or not up-to-date. Sometimes the information is two or three years old, if it's available online at all.

Another challenge is getting public records, which are not available online here in Mexico. In fact, you need special permission to request information; we don't have a law like the Freedom of Information Act in the U.S. Our new president wants to open things up through a project called E-Mexico, so maybe things will change in this country. But right now, it's very hard to get public records.

Another difficult part of research is getting information on private companies. Information on most public companies in Latin America is available, through stock exchange Web sites, for example. But finding out about private companies is very difficult, if not impossible.

When you're looking for information in a region that you are not as familiar with, how do you know where to start?

In the case of the United States and Canada, thanks to my experience with Dialog, I have a pretty good idea of where to go. My good friends and colleagues from AIIP help, too; I can usually find someone from whatever country I am researching who knows the local sources.

For sources outside North America or Latin America, it's more of a challenge. We can usually identify a few sources, thanks to the manuals and handbooks that talk about international online information sources, so we start with those. While there aren't many books in Spanish, I do use sources like the Super Searcher series [198] as well as *Find It Online* [177] and *Online Competitive Intelligence* [193]. But if the client has a specific question, then we look for somebody who can help us. For example, the other day we had a question for the French Petroleum Institute, so we had to find somebody from the petroleum industry to help us.

So, to summarize, we first go to the most official sources that we can think of, like a government office or companies that are known worldwide. From there we start looking for specific sources, and if we can find somebody to speak to, that's great.

How do you know when you have covered all the likely sources when you are working on an international research project, especially if you aren't really familiar with the sources?

When I see that the information I am finding is repeated, when I am not getting any additional information, then I know that the famous law of diminishing returns has set in. When I keep working and digging and I don't get much in return, I decide to stop. Of course, I also have to work under budget constraints; usually we work with clients who don't have an unlimited budget. They say, "Look for the information until you've spent this much." So at that point, we send them what we have and we say, "We have found this and we have spent this. Do you want us to go any further?" Usually they say, "No, I think that's enough."

And sometimes people are in urgent need of information, so time is also a constraint. If the sources are not readily available, and are not online, I tell the client that it might take a month or two to get the information. In those situations, the client will usually decide not to continue the research. We need sources that can be obtained in no more than two or three weeks.

Do you encounter any problems with copyright or privacy issues when you send information to a client outside Mexico?

Privacy is not really a big concern here yet, although we're moving toward more regulation. Copyright wasn't an issue until recently, and now it's becoming more and more important. Mexico was one of the countries that didn't care much about copyright, but now with NAFTA and globalization, more and more companies are concerned about copyright. When we provide copies of documents or articles, we always remind our clients that the information is copyrighted.

Do you run into situations where your clients are asking for information that simply isn't collected or made available in other countries?

Yes, I do. For example, I got a question from a client in the U.S. who wanted to locate somebody who had moved to Mexico, but the client didn't know where the person had moved to. That information is just not publicly available. You have huge databases in the U.S. that help you look up people's phone numbers or addresses, but we don't have that in Mexico.

Another challenge is finding information on private property, such as personal real estate. For example, a client from Texas asked us to find information about a chemical plant, along with the industrial process blueprints for the site—information on how the raw materials are processed to produce the end products. That information is not available. It may be publicly available in the States, but it's not available in my country.

So we have to manage the client's expectations. Sometimes it's very hard for them to understand that what they want just does not exist, or isn't readily available. I hate to say this, but sometimes some people even try to bribe officials to get that information. We don't do that, of course. We don't do spying, or anything like that.

There are some blind spots there, because some information is simply not available. This is the case almost everywhere in Latin America. The reference interview is a vital part of the process for us, because it helps us clarify with the client how far we can go, what kind of information we can get, how costly or inexpensive it is, how long it will take, and so on. It is so important to manage the client's expectations; we don't want to over-promise.

Related to this, I notice that many researchers in the U.S. do a lot of phone research as well as online or manual research. In Mexico, it's not as easy to get information over the phone. People have to meet you. So you make an appointment, and you visit the person, and then sometimes you still can't get a lot of information until the person knows you. Often, it's not just a matter of going to the office to talk. Sometimes you have to discuss it over a meal, and that takes even longer. But it's part of our culture.

I have a personal example of this. My sister married an American and they moved back to Mexico. My brother-in-law is frustrated; he says to me, "I do everything in the States over the phone, and here I can do almost nothing over the phone."

That's why we don't use email or postal mail to contact sources. If I need information from Venezuela or Colombia or Argentina, first I go to the Web, or to fee-based online sources or print sources. If I can't find the information there, I call or email a colleague who will go in person and get the information. It's an interesting issue; each country has its own rules, its own proto-col. Personal networking is vital in Latin America. You have to make friends before you make plans. It's a two-edged sword, because if you quarrel with your contact, then you can't get the information you need.

Do you use any country-specific search engines?

Yes. The most popular search engines for us are Yahoo! Mexico [160] and Yupi [161], which covers most of the Latin American countries and also Spain. The other one that is very good and very complete is Terra [132], from Spain.

We are seeing more and more Latin American search engines, but they are becoming more internationally focused. There's an analogy to television: More and more local television companies are going international, but you also have the Spanish equivalents of the major U.S. networks such as CNN, TNT, and NBC. If I have to find something about a specific country, first I go to the local Web search engine. After that, I go to one that is more regional or that covers the entire world. It's interesting; I find, when I teach online searching courses, that my students don't know that local sources exist. They usually go to Yahoo!, AltaVista [4], or Excite [47]—the most popular international search engines. I have to tell them that there are local search engines too.

As for other free online sources on the Web, I use Bancomext [12], the Mexican Bank for Foreign Trade; COSMOS [28], a directory of companies arranged by industry; SIEM [121], the Mexican government's business information source; IMPI [65], the National Institute for Industrial Property; and SICE [120], the Foreign Trade Information Service from the Organization of American States.

What about fee-based online services? I'm sure that you use Dialog; what other online services do you rely on for international research?

Because of my background and experience, and because of the quality of information, my first choice is Dialog. I also use STN [129] for scientific and technical searches. Sometimes I use LexisNexis, but it's not really very useful for our needs. That's another interesting cultural difference between Mexico and the U.S.: In the States, case law is very important, but in Mexico, we use the codes and the laws, and we don't focus as much on court cases. The LexisNexis people have been very frustrated, because they haven't been able to sell their product here the way they wanted to. But then they decided to put up the laws and international agreements from several Latin American countries, and now it's becoming more popular.

Unfortunately, we have very few online systems of our own in Latin America. InfoLatina [70] is pretty good, but we don't have many sources to begin with and, as I mentioned earlier, many of those sources are on CD-ROM, not online. For global searches, I use the traditional international online systems.

Fortunately, more and more library catalogues are going online, and there is more and more collaboration among libraries. There is also a project to automate interlibrary loans, which has been very successful.

How do you stay up-to-date on new information sources?

I subscribe to international publications like *Online* [192], *Searcher* [196], and *Information Today* [182], and *Information World Review* [183] for the European perspective. I also subscribe to Free Pint [178], and I read the newsletters that the online vendors send out to customers. We don't have many local magazines or journals that deal with the information industry here in Mexico. I read the local financial newspaper, *El Financiero* [176], which is the Mexican equivalent of *The Wall Street Journal*. It's very useful, because I learn about new business information sources on the Internet.

Other ways that I stay updated include attending professional conferences when I can. And the private AIIP email discussion list is wonderful. It's very, very useful, not only because you always get an answer when you put a question on it, but also for the research suggestions and new Web sites that get discussed. We have a similar email list in Mexico for librarians, called BIBLIOMEX-L [163], which I rely on.

What trends do you see in global research? What do you think you'll be doing differently in three or four years?

Well, there has been a huge growth in the number of Web sites, but unfortunately many of them are superficial in nature. They have very little information that is useful for us. But I expect that, in the next few years, the sites will be fleshed out with more useful information. Another thing that is growing now, and maybe it's just the current fashion, is portals. People are looking more at content, and focusing more on providing useful information. I think the trend is to get more content online, including converting CD-ROM products to online.

One thing that is going to take longer, because it's a cultural issue, is the process of bringing public records and other government information online. I see lots of blind spots in the online information market here in Latin America. We have very few reliable company directories, for example, and it's very hard to determine if the information we do have is reliable. We usually use either international sources like Dun & Bradstreet [36], which has its own information policies, or local or government-based directories, which we can't always rely on.

Pricing and economic issues still need a lot of work here. We still must explain to people that getting value-added research through an independent information professional will cost money. Part of the function of the reference interview is to make sure clients understand that they will have to pay for it, that it won't be free.

Super Searcher Power Tips

➤ Most of the Latin American countries are beginning to put their information online, but it's very hard to find a full Latin American database. So we have to go country by country, and we find that the quality varies from source to source, and some sources are more detailed than others.

➤ The problem with relying on government information is that it can be biased, but that's all we have.

➤ The biggest challenge is that Latin American information is just not available online, or not readily available online, or not up to date.

➤ Each country has its own rules, its own protocol. Personal networking is vital in Latin America.

Global Food Industry Experts
Maribeth Bacig

Maribeth Bacig is Manager, Client Services at Cargill Inc. in Minneapolis, Minnesota. The Information Center provides business and technical information and knowledge management services to Cargill employees worldwide.

Maribeth_Bacig@cargill.com

Peter Sidney

Peter Sidney is Assistant Vice President and Director of the Information Center at Cargill Inc. in Minneapolis.

Peter_Sidney@cargill.com

Peter and Maribeth, can you tell me a bit about your backgrounds?

PS: I went to school here in Minnesota at a small liberal arts college, and my story is probably similar to that of a number of other library science people. I majored in English and history and I thought I would be a teacher. I got into student teaching and I decided, well, this doesn't really seem like the thing for me, so then I didn't know what to do with the education I had. My wife's roommate was a library science minor, and she told me that I could go to library school and get a job in a library even if I had never worked in a library. I thought, "Well, I like research." So eventually I went to library school at the University of Maryland, and I graduated in 1979. While I was there, I landed an internship at the White House Information Center; that was my first professional library job. It was a very good thing that I started as an intern while I was in school, because I didn't like library school that much but I loved the work itself. I knew that that was what I wanted to do.

After I finished school, I got a permanent job at the White House, working for White House staff and the Office of Management and Budget. I worked there for about three years altogether. That was where I got my first exposure to reference work and to international issues. We would do work for the National Security Council and some of the foreign policy advisors, and there would be preparation work when the President went on trips. Then my wife and I moved back to Minnesota, and I got a job in the business library at Pillsbury Company, which of course is an international company, and I learned more about business reference there. Then in 1989 I came to Cargill, which is even more of an international company, so I've gotten a lot more exposure to international research and the food industry from working here.

And how about you, Maribeth?

MB: I went to library school at the University of California, Berkeley in 1986, but I actually knew I wanted to be a librarian from the time I was in high school. I'm one of these weird people. I worked in my public library in Duluth as a page and read more books than I shelved. I had received my undergraduate degree in humanities in 1984, and the job market was awful; the only jobs I could get were in retail. I worked at a knitting store and taught knitting, and I started talking to the people in my knitting classes about what they did for work. That's when I first found out about corporate librarianship; I had a couple of corporate librarians in my classes, one of whom was actually an information broker who introduced me to Roger Hurd at INFORM, the fee-based research service of the Minneapolis Public Library. In fact, I wound up working there eventually.

After talking with the information broker and some other people in Minneapolis, I looked for a library school that was very computer oriented; several schools were recommended to me by a computer programmer. The University of California, Berkeley was one of them. California was sunny and warm, it had a short program, and it was a public school. I was smart enough to know that librarians didn't make a lot of money, so I picked the cheapest place to go, which was UC, Berkeley. I had Marydee Ojala as a teacher, so I got the benefit of her expertise, and I did a little bit of international research there, just learning about some of the companies there in the San Francisco Bay Area.

Then I came back to Minneapolis and worked as a solo librarian in an environmental engineering firm. The company didn't do very well, and I ended up on the job market again. That's when I started working at INFORM, the fee-based research service within the Minneapolis Public Library. It's one of the oldest in the country; it was established back in 1970. Through my work at INFORM, I was introduced to Cargill. I spent a lot of time doing government document searching for Cargill, looking for statistics about agriculture. Cargill hired me away from INFORM in 1994, and that was where I really started to do international research.

Like Peter, I specialize in the food industry and agriculture. It's been international research from the very beginning; in fact, it seems like that's all we do at Cargill. You can't ever just look at the U.S. market; our clients always want to know what the market is for the product worldwide. So it seems like global research is something that I've done since I first came here, and it's hard for me to think about it as any different than any other type of research.

PS: This is a very global company. We have about 85,000 employees in sixty countries. About half of those people are outside the United States, but, more importantly, we are a global player in a global market. Even when we get requests from headquarters here in Minneapolis, their markets are almost all global, or at least they include a number of regions of the world. Even though most of our requests come from people within the United States, we're almost always looking at global markets. And in just about any of the industries in which we compete, we will have major competitors in Europe, Asia, and Latin America, not just in the United States.

Can you describe a typical research project?

MB: Projects that are typical—and also rather difficult to do—include questions like identifying all the companies in Asia that make soft drinks. We always look for new resources, and we're finding more print resources than electronic for that kind of question. We end up purchasing a lot of the Euromonitor [42, see Appendix] publications. We also find market research companies that specialize in international research for the food industry. For example, Seymour-Cooke [118] is a U.K.-based company that looks at the food distribution system and the players in particular countries, and their reports tell us a lot. So we rely a lot on international reports to answer those types of questions.

Other common projects are things like the market for orange juice in China. For a project like that, we tend to look for either market studies or companies that specialize in juice and beverage research. We use the Internet a lot to find market research sources. One of the hardest questions for me is determining the best sources for a particular project, especially if I find sources that I haven't used before or in a region I'm not familiar with. I email people I know in those countries, asking, "Have you ever heard of these reports? Have you seen any of them? Do you have an opinion about these reports?" In a company this size and this geographically diverse, it's hard to keep track of who has bought what. As much as we try to centralize purchasing of market research reports, it just doesn't happen. So I'll contact Cargill people in whatever region I'm researching, to see whether they have purchased the report I have identified, or anything similar.

PS: Usually, the people we contact will be people who have spent time here in Minneapolis and are now stationed at a non-U.S. location. We are part of the public affairs organization of our company, so we know public affairs people in many locations. We also make use of the staff economists in those locations; we've made some pretty good contacts with them. About eighteen months ago, Maribeth and I made a trip to some of our offices in Asia. One of the things we did while visiting the offices was an information audit to find out what sources people use, and what sources they had access to, like trade associations, market researchers, those sorts of things. We learned a fair amount from doing that, and also made contact with people there whom we could get in touch with to ask about a particular source later on. For most countries, we found that there weren't many English-language resources that we didn't already know about. We expected to hear about a lot of new sources, but most of the time we were telling them about U.S.-based information sources that they hadn't heard of before. That was reassuring, to find out that we were already using most of the good sources all along.

We recently were asked about sources for Japanese company information and Japanese news information. We're not set up to handle Japanese-language resources here, so we looked at what options would be available to us from Japan that we might not know about. I asked the public affairs contacts in Tokyo whom we had dealt with during our visit, "What resources do you know of, what do you use that we might take advantage of?" They suggested Nikkei Net [99], which I have tried, although I'm not sure that it adds much for us. In any event, it's useful to be able to ask local contacts for pointers on resources we might not have heard of here in the U.S.

Do you find that you use different research methodologies for different regions of the world?

MB: In some ways, yes. If you're talking about the U.S., Canada, and Europe, Dialog [33], LexisNexis [88] and Dow Jones Interactive [35] do a good job; they all have pretty good research sources for understanding the market for food products in those countries. For Asia and Latin America, we tend to use the Web a bit more, although I have to admit we're not a group of really big Web users, aside from sources we know and trust. For an agricultural company like Cargill, there is no better source for understanding the general agricultural and commodity markets in other countries than the Foreign Agricultural Service of the U.S. Department of Agriculture [142], which is a free service. We also contact people within the Foreign Ag Service, if we can't answer the question ourselves. We contact a lot of people to get recommendations for resources, if we're not finding what we want in the general sources out there.

PS: We haven't found much value or had much success in using Web search engines for those unfocused searches where you're just looking for something on a topic, when you don't know exactly what you're looking for or what sources you want. Rather, we identify the sources that are of use to us, and then we go directly to those sources. Sometimes they are on the Web, sometimes they aren't.

MB: If I have a little extra time, when I've gone back to one of our usual sources, I will say to myself, "All right, let's see what I would have found if I had gone searching on the Web for this information." What tends to happen is that I don't find any new information. I find the same things that I found in the sources I already used. That's encouraging; I know that I've done a better job by going to the sources that we're accustomed to using most often.

The other kinds of questions we get, which are really hard to answer from the Web, are questions like, "How much ice cream is produced in all of Europe?" Nobody asks how much ice cream is produced in France—they want to know all of Europe. Well, Europe doesn't think of itself as a single unit. Multinational companies do, but Europe itself doesn't. You just can't answer that kind of question on the Web; you have to do it country by country by country by country.

PS: And because we're looking at the whole region, we tend toward sources like Euromonitor, Datamonitor [30] and Eurostat [46]—sources that are regionwide. Europe is probably where this issue is most prominent, but to a certain extent we find it to be the case in Asia, too. But usually in Asia, we're looking at a country or a selection of countries, not the entire region as a whole.

MB: We discovered when we went to Asia that, for Chinese market information, printed sources are okay but not particularly accurate. Most of the best information comes from the people on the ground there, primary research from our own Cargill people. They've got people out looking at the crops, so they know how big the crop is going to be. They can make estimates based on their expertise and familiarity with the crop.

PS: I was surprised by the amount of published information that they're able to get on the ground in China, from universities and from trade associations. That may be the situation in other countries as well. For certain kinds of research, when we need to get into a fair amount of depth, it's pretty hard for us to deliver market information from here in Minneapolis that is as good as what they can get from published sources within the country. The information is not going to be on the Web and it's not going to be in databases.

Are there any alternatives for those of us who don't have people in-country who can obtain the information directly?

MB: There are some alternatives, but for real numbers and real information, there's a cost involved. We tend to buy as many of the statistical abstracts and similar resources produced by the countries as we can.

PS: We can get the agricultural statistics from China or from Russia, published in English. Another thing that anybody can do, although you need to allow time to get a response, is to make use of attachés at the U.S. embassies in various countries. We do a lot of communicating by email, particularly with the agricultural attachés, but also with economic and commercial attachés. You can ask them questions and they will generally do a fair amount of work, contacting people in trade associations in the country, getting you government statistics, that sort of thing. That's one resource that anybody can take advantage of, if you've got a little time to wait for a reply. If you need things immediately, it's not going to help you very much.

MB: Also, it depends on the country. They all operate on their own sense of time. Some of the Latin American countries take more time than other regions. In order to get at least some information fairly quickly, I often just ask them to steer me to the trade associations in their country that might deal with this topic, or I will ask for suggestions for other resources. I'll ask if there is somebody there who does market research for them. In those countries, you really do need to work your contacts.

Do you ever use the Industry Sector Analysis reports from Stat-USA [127] for contact names?

PS: No, I haven't used Stat-USA for that, although I've used it for statistics and all kinds of other information. We tend to use the U.S. Department of State's Key Officers List [145], which lists all the attachés at each of the U.S. embassies.

How do you think international research resources have changed in the last few years?

MB: I don't think that the publishers have really changed. However, I think that they are becoming more global in their outlook. Whereas a few years ago you would never find information on the market for juices in China, now all of a sudden there are lots of reports out there. Companies like Beverage Marketing Corporation [15], that used to produce reports only on the U.S. market, are now covering more countries. They are realizing that it's a global market, and more people are willing to buy reports on the market outside the U.S.

PS: One of the big changes I've seen has been not just in what's available, but in the ability to locate the information. For international organizations, and foreign governments for that matter, it used to be that, even if you knew something existed, it was pretty hard to get at it. You'd have to order the print copy of an International Monetary Fund [75] report, for example. You didn't have the State Department's Country Background Notes [145] and the *CIA World Factbook* [26] on the Web. You didn't have agricultural attaché reports, which are really important to us. For all that kind of information, even if you knew it existed, you had to order it and wait for it to come, or get somebody to fax it to you.

Now, the amount that's immediately available, particularly if you know it exists and know where to look for it, is pretty amazing. You can go to the United Nation's Web site [139] and get all the UN population statistics; you don't have to worry about whether you have the book in your collection. In fact, not just for international sources, but generally, the Web has made things immediately accessible that you used to have to order or get in some other way.

MB: And the information you get has been updated more frequently. For example, we are often asked for import/export statistics for commodities moving in and out of the U.S. What's hard for us is finding information about trade between other countries; there aren't as many sources for that kind of data. I was just looking at USA Trade Online [150], which contains the trade statistics that used be in the National Trade Data Bank [96]. Now, it's much more up-to-date; for example, they've already got the import/export statistics from a couple of months ago. It may get to the point where it will actually be more up-to-date than PIERS

[110], which is really fast when you compare it to the way things have been.

We've been looking at a lot of tools for finding tariff rates for different countries. This is a question we get all the time that's very difficult to answer. You see, a company like Cargill has many places where it can store, say, soybeans to sell to another country. We can sell soybeans from the U.S.; we can sell soybeans from Brazil; we can sell soybeans from Canada. We'll be asked for information to help determine the best place from which to sell soybeans into Europe or into Africa. And that depends on all the different trade rules. It would take three or four days to find out what the tariff rates would be if it came from Brazil as opposed to the U.S. or Canada.

Some of these new resources are meant for that sort of trading. However, they still don't cover the other type of question we get, which is how much steel, for example, has moved among the countries in Europe, and where has it moved from? Right now, the only source that I know of that's simple and easy to use is TradStat [137]. Otherwise, again, you have to contact a million different agencies to get the information, and you never know if they're all counting the same things the same way.

What is the most challenging part of global research? What stumps you the most?

PS: We often get requests for news or financial information about foreign companies. I've gotten questions like, "I need to know about this Korean company that declared bankruptcy. Can you get me some news stories on it? Can you get me financials?" Because we do business in English, and we are based in the U.S., and the sources we have are U.S.- and European-centric, we have a hard time with resources outside those areas. In some regions of the world, like Latin America and Asia, we'll do the search with the resources that we have, but I'll have a sense that there's some Japanese- or Korean-language database of company information that we just don't have access to that has all the information we need. But you don't really know. We have all the big-name sources like Dun & Bradstreet [36] and Teikoku Databank [131] from Japan and so forth. You search those and, if you haven't found what someone has asked you for, you don't really know if the answer is that there's nothing, or just that it's not in the sources you've been able to search.

MB: There's only one situation in which I have done any non-English-language searching. Some people in the Netherlands were looking for any mentions of a specific ship. I told them to give me the Dutch words I needed to search for, and I'd run the search through the Dutch sources on LexisNexis and Dow Jones Interactive and so on. I warned them that I couldn't do any editing of the results since I had no idea what the articles said, but they still found the material to be useful. We also have the luxury of having people around us who speak other languages, so sometimes we can get someone to translate an article that we think a client should have.

PS: And there are a few sources like Delphes [32], a marketing database with French-language abstracts and English-language indexing, so you can get at the articles by searching the indexing terms. That's one way to retrieve articles from foreign-language publications.

MB: I think what's hardest for us is that there are resources we would like to be able to search that are not covered on the online services we're using. Of course, you can find a lot of information on Europe and Latin America in the English-language databases, so even when you can go into a foreign-language database, you often don't end up finding a lot more. It's the resources that aren't on those databases that I wonder about. It is particularly a problem with Asia; I won't even attempt to search Asian characters.

Do you have any other tips for global researchers?

MB: Be sure to use your contacts. People are still one of the best sources around.

PS: When you're thinking about strategy or what the best resources might be, think about who would be interested in this information. What trade association, what government agency, market research firm, contacts in your own organization, or international agencies would care about this? Think about who would be interested and who might want to collect the information and would have the resources to do the research.

Have you encountered any difficulties in getting global site licenses for information sources that you want to provide to Cargill employees worldwide?

MB: When we made the trip to Asia and talked to vendors about a global license, they would say, "Oh yes, this is a global license." But when I asked if that meant it was okay for people in Singapore, for example, to use it, the vendor would say no. Part of it has to do with the way the vendors are structured. If you market your information products by country, and you have people who are responsible for selling your products in each of those countries, then when a customer comes to you and wants you to deliver your product to them internationally, you don't know how to compensate your employees.

PS: With one service in particular, the main impediment was that they had a sales representative in Singapore or Hong Kong, and they wanted to insist that the contract be signed separately with the Asian representative, so that the sales rep here in the U.S. wouldn't be taking the commission from the Asian person. As a result, when we visited our Asian offices, we weren't able to offer them this service because we couldn't come to an agreement on Asian site licensing through the library. We had to offer them a competing product.

When you get right down to it, though, we don't have all that many enterprise-wide licenses that are open to, say, 30,000 employees without any consideration of who would really have a use for the information. We have some resources with concurrent-user pricing, where anybody can access the service but only a certain number of people can be on at one time. And we do have some resources that are open to all users, but we keep track of how much they're being used.

Do you run into many situations where your clients presume that the information is available, but you find that the question just doesn't make sense because it's based on cultural assumptions that don't apply?

MB: Oh, yes. I had a client who wanted to know all about the food industry in Vietnam, how it works, what the market drivers are, all that sort of thing. I said, "We might be able to answer that question if they had a few more roads and phones." People assume that you can find the same kind of rich statistics for the rest of the world that you have in the U.S. Even something like gross domestic product statistics, which are the basis for how Cargill starts looking at countries, is not easy for all countries to collect. People assume that it will be readily available for all countries and that the statistics will all be in the same format and that everyone will have collected the same information.

PS: And that they will be current statistics, not from 1996.

MB: There's an assumption that every country can afford to spend money counting things, and that every country has the infrastructure to collect the data. If the country doesn't have the infrastructure of roads and telephones, it's very difficult to gather the information and make it available to researchers.

PS: As a result, sometimes the client's question just can't be answered in the same way as it would be if they asked for U.S. data. There is a perception that, because so much information is so readily available and you can find so much on the Web, that must mean that it's *all* on the Web, so why can't we find it? They don't realize that, as Maribeth said, many of these countries have no publishing infrastructure, they have no statistical infrastructure, they have no market research activities, so the information just isn't there.

Are there any other particular challenges that you run into when you're doing global research?

MB: One challenge is finding information on small, private companies. Because we are the kind of company we are, we acquire a lot of companies, so we get involved in a lot of acquisitions work. Finding information on similar acquisitions, that people can use as a basis of comparison for a proposed deal, is a true art form. A client will say, "I want to know who sold grain elevators in Brazil in the last five years." And we will think, "Oh, yeah?"

PS: Or someone will ask us to find some multiples on sales of pet food companies in Argentina.

MB: Another challenge is that there aren't any merger and acquisition databases that really meet our needs. The Worldwide Mergers, Acquisitions and Alliances database [157], which we access through the SDC Platinum CD-ROM, is okay, but it does not cover some of the start-ups that we're involved in. We are often buying just part of a company and often just a single location. Say we're buying a grain elevator or a plant: How do you compare the valuation of the purchase of a grain elevator in the U.S. with that of a grain elevator in Brazil? Most of the M&A data available does not help you to value a single plant in a foreign country. *(Editor's note: See Jan Tudor's* Super Searchers on Mergers & Acquisitions *[198])*

How do you know when to end a research project? How do you know if you have covered all the appropriate sources?

MB: Sometimes, it is determined by the budget your client gives you. We're in a charge-back situation now, which I actually prefer. I like it because it tells me how much they really want to spend trying to find this piece of information. The other way that

I know when to stop is when I start spinning my wheels. I know I've done a thorough search when the same sources keep coming up, or when everyone keeps mentioning the same contact. Then I know that I've completed the loop of what's out there. Sometimes, when I have looked at all the usual sources, then I will go out to the Internet and see if I come up with anything else. If I don't, then I feel that I have pretty much reached the limit of what is out there. Another thing that does it for us here is that there are a lot of other research questions waiting to be answered. I have to tell myself that this is all I can do on this project, I'm stopping here, and I'm going to go on to the next question. If my client wants me to do more, then he can tell me to go back and see what else I can find.

PS: We will often tell the client, "Here's what I've done, here's what I've found or not found, here's what it cost, here's what it might cost to do more. Do you want more? Is it worthwhile to go the extra mile?"

MB: And if you do continue looking, you know that you are going to spend more money and you may not find anything more.

PS: If somebody makes a request that seems unreasonable, we might say, "Well, yes, I can do this search, and I can give you the five hundred patent abstracts you want. It will cost you this amount of money. Do you want me to do that?" And they often say, "Oh my gosh, no! I had no idea it would cost that much!"

How do you stay up to date on new information resources?

PS: From time to time, we go out of our way to look for new information sources—food industry sources or company directories or other kinds of international sources.

MB: I've done that, most recently, looking for food service statistics and information, both U.S. and worldwide. It means looking for the specialized, boutique market research companies. There's not a lot out there. I spent a long time trying to put together a list of all the resources that I could find that provide this kind of service. Then I contacted other people within Cargill to find out what other services they have either purchased or have heard of that might be useful. I'm using the eyes and ears of other people within Cargill to help me find out what is available.

PS: Another example involved an economist in Singapore who has sort of a de facto information job doing research there. He put together a collection of bookmarks of Asian sources. He's shared that with us, and we've shared with him what we know about Asian and other sources. We do a lot of that kind of sharing with other people in the company.

Sometimes we get questions from clients who just want to know what information sources are available to help them with their particular needs. We have a nutraceutical business, and Japan is a big market as both a producer and a consumer of nutraceutical products. So Cargill people in Japan have been asking us where else they can find more information about the market and the companies involved.

What are your basic, can't-live-without global information sources?

MB: The Foreign Agriculture Service of the USDA, and the UN's Food and Agriculture Organization [139].

PS: Also the International Monetary Fund and the World Bank [153]. One of the sources that we subscribe to for country information is the Economist Intelligence Unit [37]. It has country reports and a newswire service. That's really valuable when we are researching the economic and political situation or considering doing business in a country. TradStat is very important to us for trade. Although PIERS only has U.S. data, it is more detailed than what you can get from the government sources.

MB: The most exciting research tools I saw at the last conference I attended were new search engines specifically for market research. USA Data [149] is good, but it focuses on U.S. information only. We also use IMR Mall [66]. MindBranch [93] is very, very cool. They do some things that I think could be very useful to us. People all over Cargill end up buying market research reports, even though we try to centralize the process. If we could get them to purchase reports through our intranet, with MindBranch we would know if someone else in Cargill had purchased a report. That could mean we could afford to purchase additional reports while not inadvertently buying duplicates of reports we already own.

I also think that World Reporter [155] is a good resource. Peter and I were just talking about it—he doesn't think it's as good as Reuters Business Briefing [115], but he hasn't been searching it lately. One of the other librarians does a lot of work on the beer market in Asia and Latin America, and she thinks that World Reporter is often a very good resource.

PS: One thing about World Reporter is that some of the records are just abstracts and not the full text. Abstracts are fine as a way of alerting you to an issue, but I get annoyed when I do a database search and pull up abstracts. What do you do with them, other than give the client the abstracts? Then it gets to be a big process to get the full text of the articles if the client wants them.

How do you think international research will have changed in three years? What will you be doing differently?

PS: I would expect that there will be even more information immediately available. However, I think that some areas of the world that we care about, such as Africa and Latin America, will still be problematic in the sense that there isn't the infrastructure in place to publish things.

MB: I think one of the true challenges for us, considering where Cargill is in the chain of manufacturing and in the food chain, is that when a country starts to become more developed and the market begins to grow, we are often the first to bring products into the country. Hence, there's always a dearth of information for whatever we're trying to do in those countries. By the time there's lots of information available, we're already established in the country. It's when we're establishing our initial foothold that we need the information, and at that point it's not available.

PS: We'll see a continuing trend toward our clients doing more on their own, whether they are here in the U.S. or in China or Singapore. They will have some Internet resources available to them and some of the information will be focused on their region or their country, in their language. We'll end up getting the more challenging questions, so it won't get any easier for us.

MB: What we've started to see lately is that people are sharing more. What I would like to see happen in the next three years is that we do a better job of capturing what we know, within Cargill. The information within our company—what we know about what's happening around the world in the food industry—is as valuable as, if not more valuable than, anything we can purchase on the outside.

PS: The way it tends to get done now is that people share information by email, so you get these emails with forwarded messages that are five pages long, and you have to read backwards through the whole thing to find out what it was originally about, and you've got ten people copied on every message. It's this proliferation of noise that doesn't capture very effectively what people know.

Super Searcher Power Tips

➤ Make use of attachés at the U.S. embassies in various countries. You can email them questions and they will generally do a fair amount of work, contacting people in trade associations or getting you government statistics.

➤ We haven't found much value or success in using Web search engines for most searches. Rather, we identify the sources that are of use to us and then we go to those sources directly.

➤   There are resources that we would like to be able to search that are not on any of the online services we're using. It's the resources that aren't on those databases that I worry about.

➤   The information within our company—what we know about what's happening around the world in the food industry—is as valuable as, if not more valuable than, anything we can purchase on the outside.

Kyoko Toyoda
Asian Business Research Expert

At the time of this interview, Kyoko Toyoda was Manager of the Business Research Center at JP Morgan in Tokyo. She now works as Director at System Development, Co. Ltd. in Tokyo. This interview was conducted via email.

k.toyoda@systemk.co.jp
www.systemk.co.jp

Can you tell me a bit about your background?

I started out as a reporter for a trade journal in Japan that is equivalent to *Publishers' Weekly* in the U.S. I realized that I needed greater proficiency in English, so in 1989 I quit my job and went to Boston University to study English. One day, I was discussing my career plan with my tutor, and she recommended that I go to a library school. "I'm not interested in libraries," I said. "What I'm interested in are databases, new ways of information dissemination, and the future of publications." And she said, "That's what library schools are teaching now." At first I was skeptical, but eventually I was convinced to apply for admission at Simmons College in Boston, where I discovered that she was absolutely right. I graduated from Simmons in 1991. After receiving some training at JP Morgan's headquarters in New York, I came back to Japan in 1992 to start a library in the Tokyo office of JP Morgan. I started the library as a solo librarian. Nine years later, it has grown to a staff of four, including myself.

How much of your work focuses on international research?

It depends on how you define "international" research. About 95 percent of our users are in Tokyo and 70 percent of our research is related to Japan. But this information often has to be prepared for the client in English in order to share it with non-Japanese speakers, including regional managers and overseas colleagues. And since we work for a company whose operations are global, we always need to consider presenting the information in a "global" way, even when we are dealing with domestic Japanese information.

JP Morgan has seven Business Research Centers worldwide—in New York, London, Frankfurt, Paris, Hong Kong, Sydney, and Tokyo. Whenever one of the other BRCs receives a Japanese-related inquiry, they pass it to us. End-users are more selfish, in a way; for example, people in the New York office might want information at 11:00 P.M., when the New York BRC has already closed. But they don't want to wait until the next morning, so they call us in Tokyo and ask for a news search on Nexis [98, see Appendix], for example. And I know that people in Tokyo are also doing the same things at other Business Research Centers when ours is closed.

Can you describe a "typical" global research project?

One example is finding all the producers of industrial gases, and comparing their market shares. Here is how I would approach this project: First, I would go to Bureau van Dijk's Global Researcher [57] database on CD-ROM. I would screen all listed companies worldwide with the SIC code of industrial gases. Then I would identify their sales volume for the product by looking up the segment data of each company's financial statement. Next, I would go to Research Bank Web [135], Profound [111] or the PROMT [112] file on Dialog [33], if I could not find the segment data in the company's financial report, or if

I needed to estimate the size of the market around the world or retrieve some background information on industry trends.

Another example of a typical global research project is getting information on historical market capitalization of all the major stock exchanges. For this, I would first go to our Bloomberg [17] terminal, which covers the market cap of most major stock exchanges. If the requester wanted more stock exchanges than what Bloomberg covers, we would try a Web search. For example, you can get a Chinese market cap at the Web site of the China Chamber of International Commerce [23] . That is probably all I could do for a requester in one day. If the requester still wanted more data, I would ask other local Business Research Centers for help, or I would purchase the fact book of the appropriate stock exchange(s), or ask the stock exchange directly about the availability of the data.

What changes have you seen in international research resources over the past few years?

There is no question that the Internet has given us a great power to access information. Say someone wants an Asian company's annual report. Until a couple of years ago, if we could not locate one on Primark's Global Access [54], we would likely have given up further searching. But now, we will try the company's home page, some Asian portal sites, and other online sources, because we've learned that there is a pretty good chance that we will find it somewhere on the Net.

Do you have any sites in particular that you could recommend?

IR Asia [77] is a useful site for locating Hong Kong and other Asian companies' annual reports. AllKorea [2], which is in Japanese, can be used to access information on Korean companies. You cannot get annual reports, but you can see profiles of Chinese companies at CCPIT [23]. Perfect Information [109] is a fee-based, online document delivery service that is quite useful for getting information on European companies, but it often has information on Asian companies as well.

Of course, you can also use Yahoo! [160] to find the company's home page and look there. It is becoming more and more likely that the company will have made its annual reports and other financial information available on the Net. This is mainly because of U.S. disclosure rules and the fact that we can all access these company reports on the Net. This has created a so-called "Global Standard" for disclosure and has indirectly persuaded Japanese and Asian governments and corporations to disclose more of their information on the Net. This has been the greatest benefit of the Internet, and we all share in the benefits.

I don't have exact figures, but I would say that half of all listed companies in Japan have English versions of their Web pages. The percentage in Hong Kong is probably higher, and the number of Korean company Web sites in English is probably lower, but getting better. In other parts of Asia, the percentage is probably still very low, say about 10 percent, but major companies do have their sites in English. Needless to say, publishing the annual report in English is not required in any Asian country. Only a few companies used to do so, and it would consist of only thirty pages or so and be published many months after the fiscal year-end. Now, their English-language content is much richer, and we may be able to get it as early as two months after the end of the fiscal year.

What is the biggest challenge you encounter when conducting global research? And what do you do to get around that challenge?

Most Asian and some European information is still not easy to locate, especially laws, regulations, accounting standards, and anything that requires background knowledge in the field. If I encounter a problem like that, I would search for a subject-matter expert within JP Morgan to give me guidance. Regarding laws and regulations, I would call a local embassy and ask for assistance. As for accounting standards, accounting firms such as PricewaterhouseCoopers and Arthur Andersen are helpful, and I call them often.

How do you deal with using sources or search tools in a language you aren't fluent in?

I can't handle search tools in any foreign language except English. As long as the interface is in either Japanese or English, I can retrieve a document such as an annual report, even if it itself is written in an unfamiliar language. At the least, I could get a corporate profile for the requester.

Do you run into problems when you are searching for information across borders?

Yes, this is the problem we often encounter, and this is one of the reasons why I said earlier that we always need to consider the global aspects of research, even when dealing with domestic information. You expect the same level of information in other countries as that which you can get in your own country. A requester thinks it should be easy to get certain information from another country, because it is so commonly available in his or her country. But this is not always true.

Let me give you some examples. You can easily search to see whether a company has been involved in legal cases in the U.S., but this information is not generally disclosed in other countries, including Japan. On the other hand, a corporate structure or organization chart must be submitted for every listed company in Japan, but you can't expect to find the same information for most companies outside Japan. We have a very good source that illustrates market shares of every product in Japan, *Market Share in Japan* [190], but you shouldn't take it for granted that an equivalent source exists in other countries.

But you don't always know the reason why you are having trouble locating a certain piece of information until you have some expertise and experience in researching the country or region. Maybe you are not finding the information because of a regulation, or maybe it is a matter of business custom, or perhaps it is simply the lack of a research source that provides relevant information, or maybe the way you are searching is just not right. It is hard to tell sometimes.

This points out the importance of networking. Our job is to become an expert on Japanese information and to become savvy about its availability, contents, unique sources, drawbacks, distribution channels, and so on, and to prevent the requesters from wasting their time searching for the wrong data or in the wrong way.

Do you license the same information for the BRCs throughout the world, or do you license information country by country? Do you have problems getting at licensed information?

I'm not the person responsible for licensing, but yes, at times I have experienced some difficulties with global licenses. For example, a vendor offers a product for global use within JP Morgan at, say, $1,000 per user per month. But 70 percent of the product consists of North American sources. If you use the database all the time, $1,000 would make sense, but it does not make sense if you only use it once a month. If a vendor wishes to expand its market globally, it should either make the product's contents more globally focused or offer a good discount for overseas markets. But what usually happens is that vendors *say* their product is global enough because of the 30 percent of the content that is non-North American, and they try to get our New York contact to sell the product globally within the firm. It is very hard for me, however, to find a reason to join the contract. From my standpoint, joining a global contract is justified only when it brings us extensive access to information resources at a cheaper price than what we would have received from dealing with the vendor locally.

Are there any other challenges that you often encounter when doing global research?

Time pressure. If a requester gives us sufficient time, we can try lots of approaches, but they often come to us in a rush and say they need it within a day! Because of time zone differences, contacting someone in another region may not happen immediately, and we may need to wait overnight to receive a response. At times, I need to stay late, come in early, or even make a phone call from home to make sure someone received my inquiry and in order to get a response quickly.

The four of us in the Tokyo Business Research Center receive forty to fifty requests per day. Once every two or three days, we aren't able to complete a request locally and have to pass it on to other people or another office. Once every two or three months, I have to place an international phone call to make sure that they can find the information we need. Sometimes, despite my worry, they say that what we asked for was easy; then the phone call ends in a minute. Other times, they say that what we are asking for would be hard to find; then we need to discuss alternatives. I explain the purpose of the research and ask for professional advice, so I know what I can expect to receive within the next couple of days.

Do you have the impression that there is more of an expectation that you can get information immediately, now that "everything is on the Web" and "everyone is on email"?

Regarding Japanese or Asian information, yes, they believe that everything can be found on the Web and can be retrieved in minutes, although in fact much information is still only in print format. Regarding U.S. information, however, at times we need to explain to our requesters the opposite situation. For example, someone wanted to see news articles about a company in the U.S., so we tried Dow Jones Interactive [35], Nexis, and Northern

Light [100], without much success. The requester then asked us to contact the New York BRC, hoping that they might have local resources to find more news articles. They didn't realize that most U.S. publications are now on the Web or on the fee-based online services, which means there is not much difference between what a U.S. BRC would do and what we did from Japan. In other words, there are fewer and fewer truly "local" sources in the U.S. But some people don't recognize this change and still think that there must be more information outside the digital world and you can get it if you ask a local American.

How do you know when you have done a thorough search on a global topic? How do you know when to stop?

Generally speaking, the deadline that the requester gives stops me from further searching. When the research is too important to stop in the middle, and if I don't have confidence in the results I have found so far, I usually send emails to our regional branches or offices and ask for advice as to whether I have used the best sources, or whether there are other sources I should look at as well. If there's no office in the region that I am researching, I might send an inquiry to a local embassy of the country, or the Japanese Chamber of Commerce in the country, or a stock exchange, and so on. You can never be certain how complete an answer you have until you contact a regional expert.

Do you have any suggestions on how to find the appropriate contact within a local embassy, chamber of commerce, stock exchange, etc.? Do you generally find them to be helpful and responsive?

For the local embassies, you can just call the number in the phone book. And most major cities in the world have Japanese Chambers of Commerce to support the local

Japanese corporations. For example, say I would like to know about a Brazilian regulation. I might call the Brazilian embassy in Tokyo or the Japanese Chamber of Commerce in São Paulo. The good thing about the Japanese Chambers of Commerce is that they are familiar with both Brazil and Japan, so I could ask about the Brazilian regulation in comparison with the Japanese one. We could even talk in Japanese! So it's a much easier conversation for me, as you can imagine.

How helpful are they? That really depends. One suggestion I have is that you always get a better response if you make a phone call rather than sending an email or a fax. Interactive communication is essential if you want to learn about something you're not familiar with.

Because of the nature of our business, we sometimes also contact stock exchanges to obtain statistics, clarify a fact, or something like that. But generally speaking, these are much more specific and straightforward requests, so they are not very difficult to answer.

Do you use many of the country-specific search engines on the Web? If so, which ones?

For Japanese information, yes, I use Japanese search engines, including Yahoo! Japan [160], Goo [58], InfoNavigator [71] and AIM [1]. As for the rest of the world, I rely on the American or international search engines. Two that I don't use frequently, but which could be useful for non-Japanese speakers since they're in English, are J Guide [79] and the Japan Information Network [80].

Some useful sites for global information include Country Library [29], Ernst & Young International [41], IndustryLink [67], World Law [154], IR Asia, and the Asian Development Bank [11].

What fee-based online sources do you consider essential for global researchers?

For general research, the essential sources are Reuters Business Briefing [115], Dialog, and DataStar [31]. I generally prefer RBB, although if the search is in the pharmaceutical or chemical industry, I would go to Dialog or DataStar.

For Japanese research, we use a dozen Japanese databases. The major Japanese databases I use include Nikkei [99] for news searches, EL Net [38] for journal retrieval, Teikoku Databank [131] and Tokyo Shoko Research [136] for unlisted company info, and several specialized Japanese-language services.

What trends do you see in global research? What do you think you will be doing differently in, say, three years?

I don't think the language barrier will be gone, but maybe we will be able to switch the user interface more easily from one language to another. We will, of course, be able to search multi-language sources together and run machine translation if necessary to browse headlines.

Accounting formats, industrial statistical data, and so on will be more internationally standardized and one single source will provide global data, just like the economic data is standardized now. For example, the International Monetary Fund [75] provides data on GDP, unemployment rates, consumer price indexes, government deficits, export and import volumes, and so on for 180 countries. I know there are small differences in how, say, unemployment is measured from one country to the next, but still, I would say it is standardized enough to make an international comparison. I wish we could do the same thing in corporate financial analysis and industrial statistics.

What other "Super Searcher" pointers do you have on the topic of global research?

Attending an international conference offers great opportunities to expose yourself to foreign resources and learn about the current state of information in other countries. And learning about foreign information will help you understand your own country's position and its uniqueness. Any foreign conference can be helpful; I myself love the Special Libraries Association's annual conference [215], EBIC [209], and the Online Information conference [212] in London.

But, to be honest, I don't believe it is really possible to do "global research." Our management often raises the question of the feasibility of centralizing all the research centers worldwide into a single location, and having that location conduct research to provide information services globally. My answer to that is always "no." Maybe in thirty years, but it is definitely not feasible now. To research, you deal with people, culture, regulations, and structures. You can't take a single approach to research diverse cultures and societies, and you can't become an expert on hundreds of different cultures—unless you're a super genius!

You should acquire a global perspective, but you can only become an expert on your own culture. If you need to research another country, you need an expert on that country, and if you need to research globally, you need a global network of experts. If every component of the network has a global perspective, you can communicate with each other and the global research can be done.

Super Searcher Power Tips

➤ U.S. disclosure rules have created a so-called "Global Standard" for disclosure and has indirectly persuaded Japanese and Asian governments and corporations to disclose more of their information on the Net.

➤ You don't always know the reason why you are having trouble locating a certain piece of information until you have some expertise and experience in researching the country or region.

➤ When you have to contact local sources, you always get a better response if you make a phone call rather than sending an email or a fax. Interactive communication is essential if you want to learn about something you're not familiar with.

➤ Attending an international conference is a great chance to expose yourself to foreign resources and learn about the current state of information in other countries. And learning about foreign information will help you understand your own country's position and its uniqueness.

Richard Reynen
Worldwide Intranet Content Manager

Richard Reynen is a senior manager of strategic research at Deloitte & Touche, based in Minneapolis, Minnesota. He is responsible for the identification, evaluation, acquisition, and implementation of external content for intranet applications for the global firm.

rreynen@deloitte.com
www.deloitte.com

Can you tell me about your background?

I received my master's degree in library science from the University of Minnesota in 1984. I started with Deloitte & Touche in 1976, so I've been with the company for twenty-five years. Until about two years ago, I was responsible for the research information center for the Minneapolis office, doing research for the consulting, audit, tax, and human benefits divisions here in Minneapolis. At that point, I began working with the company's global intranet group, to enable our people around the world to do some searching on their own. We created an internal system that we've called Intellinet. It is a completely Web-based system—a portal—in which we've put information from a wide variety of vendors and sources. We have divided it into a number of different areas, so people can find company, industry, and country information as well as information on specific topics like e-commerce. It is a company-wide resource, and our mission is to offer information that can be used by any of our employees worldwide, twenty-four hours a day, seven days a week.

Our analysts use the site daily; it's used a lot for prospective business research, and also in their daily consulting work for clients. My guess is that about half the users are in the U.S. and half in the rest of the world. Of course, we have a network of research centers around the world, but the Intellinet system is designed to enable the analysts to get quite a bit of information on their own. If they need more in-depth research, they're referred back to the specialists in these research centers. If they want just a little bit of information about a company—financials and that sort of thing—this would take care of it, but if they really want to do a complete analysis and get everything that's been published, then they can turn it over to our researchers.

Because of Intellinet, we get fewer of the really broad, unfocused questions, because the analysts are able to do some initial research to educate themselves about the topic. What we're seeing in the research center are more specific requests for information. I think the research is a lot tougher now because, once they have an overview, they want to dig deeper, so they ask for really specific information. That's what's tough for our researchers, trying to get that little nugget of information. We used to be able to wow them by getting them basic information on a subject. We can't wow them anymore, because the questions are getting harder, but the turnaround time is still the same. They still need it now. If I had the time, I could probably find all those last little bits of information, but sometimes it takes more time. That's why I got out of the research center and moved into the development of the intranet portal; it was just so frustrating.

Have you encountered the problem of people thinking they can do all their own research and, as a result, not calling the library?

Yes, there's still that mentality. We hire a lot of people right out of graduate school, and I think they assume that they can do it all, that they're doing it well. A lot of times, they'll spend eight hours trying to find something. If they don't find it, then they come to us. Of course, we can find it quickly, and they wonder, "How did you do that?" They're still using the popular search engines and wasting their time, not focusing their search right to the point. So, in the new-employee orientation, we try to stress that we have this tool, Intellinet, but that if they want to spend their time wisely, they should come to the research centers first. Sometimes I wish that the Internet had a timer on it; if it takes you more than fifteen minutes to find something, it shuts down and tells you to go call the research center.

I agree! Tell me more about the intranet portal that you make available to your end-users.

What we've done is categorize the types of information that people generally look for—company information, industry information, and country information—and then, within those categories, we've identified vendors that offer that information along with intuitive user interfaces that people can understand without training. Once we've identified the vendors, then we negotiate contracts for global access to those databases. We have a front end that verifies the users as Deloitte employees, and then takes them out to the vendor site.

When it's appropriate, we use the intranet "toolkits" that the online vendors provide. For example, we work with Factiva [48, see Appendix] to do our news feed. It lets us bring the news in past our firewall and provide a customizable news segment, so that people can select the companies and industries to monitor.

How did you go about building the Intellinet site?

Obviously, it's never going to be 100 percent perfect, and it'll never really be finished. It started out with people's need to get new clients. They wanted a quick way to get company profiles and related information, so we started with OneSource [102], then built from there. It's great to have a good overview from OneSource or Hoover's [64] and then bring in all the other pieces of the puzzle. We look for vendors that are strong in certain areas—company information or international trade information. We needed to get country information, the rules and regulations of different countries and that type of thing, because that's of interest to our clients when they go global. So we have included sources from vendors as well as links to sources on the open Web.

We used a lot of meta-sites to find global information, including Asian Business Watch [10] and Latin World [86]. I recently came across WorldSkip [156], which leads you to resources within a country, including information on the embassies, on doing business in the country, that type of thing. Meta-sites like those have been very helpful to us. I also refer people to Brint [18], a portal site that focuses on e-business and knowledge management, depending on the subject.

What online sources do you consider critical to any international business researcher's tool kit?

For country and company information, we use Global Access [54]; that's a key product for us. The Bureau van Dijk [19] suite of products is very good, especially for international researchers. I think that Amadeus [6] is very important to our European people. For country information, EIU [37] is really good. Other country information is available through the U.S. State Department [145], but I don't know if that's always current. We're always interested in very current, up-to-date information, and a lot of the government statistical sources just don't work under the same timelines that we do.

How do you evaluate a Web site for inclusion in your portal, particularly sites that you're not already familiar with?

A lot of times, we rely on the recommendations of our research people in the field, in the geographic area that's covered by the site. The problem we had with doing international research was identifying sources outside the U.S. Since I'm based in the U.S., I was more familiar with the sources here, and not as familiar with the techniques for finding company information in France or Belgium. So we've relied on our people over there to recommend the sources and Web sites that they use regularly. We're fortunate in that we are part of a global company. But even if I wasn't in a global organization like this, I probably would be smart enough to contact librarians in France or wherever if I was really stumped. It's important to find some contacts in the region that you're researching.

Can you tell me what online products you've got on the intranet portal?

I'd love to share this, but our field is so competitive. While we cooperate with our colleagues in other Big Five accounting firms, I'm sure they would never let me see what they have on their internal sites, and I can't do that either.

That makes sense. What particular challenges have you run into in building the portal?

My biggest challenge is getting sources that everybody can be happy with. Of course, there's the language issue. The official language of the firm is English and I believe that all partners and managers within the firm do speak English. But the people who really need to use the information are lower down in the organization, and they don't always speak English. We've tried to incorporate some multilingual resources into our system; we have sources from Latin America in Spanish or Portuguese, for example.

The other frustration is the lack of consistency in the data that's available. I think that's the biggest stumbling block, especially in a company like ours, which deals with financial information. The reporting requirements are different in every country, but there's an expectation that you're going to be able to compare apples to apples, and that's not always the case. In the U.K., for example, the financials are quite detailed and they have such strict reporting requirements that you can find out pretty much anything about the company. You don't have those requirements in the U.S. and some other countries, so you don't get that level of detail.

We try to highlight problems like these when we give people the information. I know that OneSource in particular is working to develop tools to enable users to compare the companies' financials. They try to massage the data to make it more standardized, so that you could do a spreadsheet comparing companies internationally within an industry.

Another challenge is that, when you're dealing with European companies, the annual reports may not be as current as they are in the U.S. They have something like a year to file their financials, whereas the U.S. requires that the annual financials be reported within ninety days. So people often complain that the data is too old. It's a challenge to have to say to them, "Well, they can do it whenever they feel like it in some counties."

Even though we're using commercial vendors for the intranet site, a lot of people think that we're putting the data in ourselves. The biggest question we get is, "Where's the data coming from? Who's putting this in here and why is it so late?" We're really at the mercy of the vendors, but we are the ones who hear the complaints.

How have you seen online resources change over the last few years?

The impact of the Web, of course, has been tremendous. You see a lot more information accessible there, but you also see the commercial vendors expanding their coverage globally. Dow Jones Interactive [35], for example, seems to be getting more international content recently, and more in-depth information. There's more of a hunger for international information, so that's spurring companies to go out and compile that material and put it together in a database. There's finally enough of a worldwide market to make it worth creating a good online resource. One example is the Latin American market, which was so under-served for years; it is finally growing. With U.S. companies looking for new markets and needing current information on Latin America, more vendors are gathering that information than in years past.

Designing the kind of international intranet portal we have now would have been a lot more challenging five or six years ago. Even when we started this project a couple of years ago, a lot of vendors were still CD-ROM-based and wanted us to load their data directly on the server. Although we wanted the information, we told them, "Sorry, we're not going to put it up on our server. We want everything totally Web based." These days, we still sometimes run into vendors, particularly outside the U.S., that haven't migrated their data to the Web, so we just can't use it.

I know that vendors in some countries have a hard time because their telecommunications system is so poor. Their local customers experience really slow download times, so they prefer CD-ROM, which isn't dependent on a reliable telecom infra-structure. Also, some countries have specific vendors that have that whole market sewn up; one product pretty much dominates the market, and they focus all their marketing efforts within the country. If we try to purchase the product, they put an enormous price on it.

Have you had problems negotiating global contracts with vendors?

Yes, the sales organizations for some of these vendors are still organized by geographic area. It's hard to get a global contract because you have to get the consent of all these different sales reps around the world, and they all need their cut. That's always a big problem. We've played hardball with them a lot of times; if they wanted our business, they were going to have to meet our requirements. We've gotten them to do that to some extent; we tell them that we don't want to worry about how they're going to compensate their sales reps. We haven't had to give up a source because of this, fortunately; they want the Deloitte & Touche business, so they're willing to accommodate us.

Another problem I run into is contracts based on the number of employees in the firm. That type of pricing model makes no sense, because not all the employees use a specific product, and certainly not all the time. This is especially the case when you get into more specific sources, like mergers and acquisitions data sources. Not everybody's doing M&A work, only a small subset, so if we're charged on a per-employee basis, that's not really fair. We try to negotiate concurrent-user pricing instead, which is more equitable.

One other problem with developing this type of intranet portal is that, once you put the stuff up, it's hard to take it away from people. If we were to put, say, Dow Jones Interactive on the system and then take it away later, our people would really complain. So you have to be careful how you negotiate with the vendor, because in a way you're signing up for life. You know how contracts can be; they lure you in with a cheap price and then they keep increasing the price as you go on. Eventually it becomes cost prohibitive.

Related to contracts is the challenge of finding sources that satisfy people in all the countries where Deloitte & Touche has offices. For example, the office in France might want a certain set of resources, but of course, people in France would probably be the only ones using it. We haven't really worked out a mechanism to be able to block access so that we can only pay for access from a single country. It's a balancing act; we've got to go back to the philosophy of what we're trying to do. We're trying to provide a good selection of material for everyone, but not in-depth resources for everything for every country and every industry. That's why we refer people back to their research center and tell them, "If you really want to get these sources, you should have them available in your local research center."

How do you stay updated on new online resources?

That's a tough one. We read *CyberSkeptic's Guide* [169], *Information Advisor* [181], those sorts of magazines. We also subscribe to Outsell's [105] consulting service. It is pretty much U.S.-focused, but their inquiry service can be helpful. It's really mostly our own internal network that keeps us informed. We've had a lot of suggestions from people within Deloitte, saying "How about this," or "Have you looked at that?"

What trends do you see for the next few years regarding international research?

We're going to see more aggregation of content through single portals. I expect to see a real shift in which everything is put together for you. People don't want to go and get the pieces of information they need from lots of different sources; they want all the pieces in one place. If a librarian wants to know something about General Motors, for example, he's willing to go to one place for financials, then another place for news articles, and a third place for research analyst reports, and so on, in order to piece it all together. But most people just want to be able to type in "GM" and then retrieve a single document with all these pieces already in one place. That's where we're going to see the shift in terms of delivery of information. We're doing some of that in our intranet, and we're working toward having a single template to present the information. But right now we still have a piecemeal system. Librarians are tolerant of that, but our end-users aren't.

Related to that, I see a shift in how the research centers deliver information to the end-users. For years, we've just kind of gathered the information and thrown it at them and said, "Here's your stuff—you read it, and make your own decisions." Now they want us to digest it and put it in a nice format. That extra analysis is what they want to see on the intranet portal site as well.

Super Searcher Power Tips

➤ It's important to find contacts in the region that you're researching, to get leads to reliable sites and resources.

➤ For country and company information, we use EIU and Global Access. The Bureau van Dijk suite of products is very good, and Amadeus is very important to our European people.

➤ You have to be careful in your negotiations with vendors, because you're signing up for life. If you put a system up on an intranet and then take it away later, people will really complain.

➤ We used to just gather the information and throw it at the clients. Now, we are providing analysis as well, and that's what they want to see on the intranet portal site, too.

Valerie Matarese

Biochemist Turned Italian-Information Provider

Valerie Matarese is the president of Up To info technologies in Pieve di Soligo, a town in northeastern Italy. Up To i.t. offers information research and analysis, focusing on information about Italy and specializing in biomedicine.

vmatarese@uptoit.org
www.uptoit.org

To start, can you tell me about how you wound up starting your business and what you do now?

My university training was in laboratory research, in biochemistry, and I have degrees from universities in NewYork and Minnesota. In the U.S., I worked in academic research environments on both coasts, and I worked in industrial research here in Italy for five years before changing careers. I can cite a few issues that led me to change from bench research to information research. The first issue is that research in biochemistry and molecular biology depends heavily on bio-informatics. By that I mean the databases and software to organize and manipulate molecular information. So, for my research, I was working remotely on large databases using command language for VAX and UNIX, and I imagine that's like what searching classic Dialog [33, see Appendix] was like. So there is a parallel between the field of biomedical research and the information industry, and that was the part of the research that I really enjoyed.

The second reason I changed careers is related to the fact that I moved to Italy for personal reasons, and took at job at Glaxo Wellcome, which has a research center in Verona. I found *Online* [192] and *Database* (now *EContent* [172]) magazines in the library there. I started to read them, and I realized how different the information industry was in Italy as compared with the United States. I was reading mostly about what was going on in the States and seeing what wasn't available locally, even though I was at Glaxo, which is a corporate leader in using information in Italy. So I imagined there would be future developments in Italy that I could participate in, and that gave me the idea to leave bench research and start an independent information research company.

We founded Up To info technologies, which we call Up To i.t., about four years ago, with the goals of promoting awareness and use of information and critical thinking skills. We offer information research, data analysis, and technical editing, which I think are all part of information services. Glaxo and the other major research centers in Italy were far from my home, and so, instead of moving to an industrialized area, I invented a job that I could do in a more natural environment, and that seems to be working out. We're in a beautiful part of the country; there's less smog and we are close to the mountains. That was a personal choice, and I think that this is an activity you can do almost wherever you want.

Our clients who request information about Italy are primarily non-Italian companies located in North America and Europe. Most of our clients are other information researchers, management consulting firms, or research groups inside large corporations, although we have also been contacted by end-users.

Can you describe a typical project?

Clients tend to want an overview of a certain market in Italy— perhaps they want us to identify the most important companies in an industry, obtain contact and financial information, news and anecdotes about the industry, market statistics, product descriptions—a bit of everything on a sector. So I collect the information and write it up into a document that explains what it might mean and how it might be interpreted. I see myself as a generalist because of the various types of research I do, but a generalist for a specific field, and that's Italy.

What changes have you seen in online information products over the last few years?

Since I've been monitoring the information industry in Italy and the databases that are available, I've seen a number of positive changes. For example, the number and variety of databases and documents available have dramatically increased. Some databases have recently become available for free; they're supported by advertising or public funding. Other databases that were very costly are now less costly or free. The market is generally broadening, the offers are getting better, and prices are coming down.

So, basically, I see an overall improvement in what information can be obtained, both on the Internet and through fee-based databases. A number of Italian CD-ROM products have migrated to the Internet, some have disappeared and some have had price reductions now that they're facing competition from Internet-based sources. Periodicals are beginning to make their archives available, and starting to offer simple search features on their Web sites, although we don't have a professional collection of newspaper archives or periodical literature databases yet.

The first Italian databases that I found were oriented toward commerce and the legal sector, and now these sectors are pretty well covered. More recently, we're seeing new databases in other areas, like the environment, education, and social sciences, so we're rounding out the offerings, and that's good news. On the corporate side, several smaller database producers have been bought out by one large telecommunications company, SEAT Pagine Gialle. Traditionally, SEAT produced the Yellow Pages and industry yearbooks, but now it is expanding nationally and internationally. SEAT has bought various Italian database producers, and even owns Virgilio [151], the major Yahoo!-like Web catalog and search engine. So the Italian information industry is similar to that in the United States, where there are many mergers and acquisitions.

As for Italian commercial, high-end databases, these have come down in price. For example, I can think of one database in which certain search features were restricted to major clients who would make large down payments. The vendor distinguished between major clients and minor clients. The underlying data resources were the same; it was just that the search tools and interfaces were different. Now they have abandoned that distinction, and that's very nice. The market's changing; there is more competition.

What are the biggest challenges that you find when you're doing research?

The biggest challenge is not being able to find the information because of the lack of good databases. So much information is still not available online. Searching involves perseverance and telephoning. I use the Internet to get a bearing on a topic, to understand the issues, to find names of experts or associations, but then I have to follow them up with telephone contacts in order to identify useful documents.

For example, I wanted to understand trends in law school graduates, whether the number was increasing or decreasing. I found statistics online, but I needed to understand why the numbers were what they were. There was no periodicals database that would have led me to articles on this topic, and it's not the sort of thing that would be in the newspapers, so an Internet search would not have been useful. I arranged an appointment with the director of a bar association, and as we talked she pulled out articles that she had read and archived. So, to identify articles that are untraceable through the data banks, you have to go through contacts. That's frustrating, because it makes the research process much more difficult.

A related problem regarding information research in Italy is that information tends to not be where you expect to find it. I thought of this because, in *Super Searchers Do Business* [199], many people said that when they start a search, they think of who would have the information, where it would most likely be published. That doesn't always work here, because the people who have the information are not always willing to give it out. So you have to go around and find the information from unlikely sources.

I've found that to be the case here in the U.S. as well. And this makes it a lot more difficult to know how to start, doesn't it?

Yes. For example, I needed to find out how many judges there were in Italy. The Ministry of Justice would be the most likely source, but they wouldn't give me the answer over the phone. They required a written request, to which they did not respond. So I got the answer from the judges' pension fund. Sometimes, you just have to go around the logical source.

Another time, I needed to identify all the bureaucratic procedures required to initiate any industrial activity in Italy. I talked to a trade association, which told me that it was too complex to be explained in any one source. I figured that the Ministry of Industry should know this, but I knew that I would not get very far by asking such a broad question. So, my solution was AltaVista [4]. Writing the right search string, in Italian, I found a small city—which I've never heard of—that had published all the Ministry of Industry's documents on the topic on its Web site. I found a flow chart, all the authorization procedures, and a set of Word documents, all coming from the Ministry of Industry on each phase of the project—from building concessions to environmental impact to occupational safety. Bingo! And in the most obscure place.

I've really had some successes with AltaVista, writing specific search strings and finding obscure Web sites where information has been posted. I know that many Super Searchers use Dialog's Dialindex to identify an unlikely source, but I don't think that would be so useful here. I found that AltaVista has been strong in turning up unlikely sources on the Internet. Lately I am also getting good results using Google [59].

There's one other problem with information research in Italy that's a little unusual, and that's what I call "information diffidence." When I telephone people during my research, they are surprised that I do this kind of work. They're not familiar with it, and while some are pleasantly surprised and ask questions about it and are supportive, other people are incredulous and afraid to talk on the phone. If I call an association and ask for an innocuous piece of information, they may be afraid to respond for "privacy reasons." They're not used to this type of questioning or this kind of research. We're still at the stage where, if you tell someone you do online research, it doesn't have a lot of meaning. In the States, you've overcome that problem.

How do laws regarding privacy or copyright affect how you do your research?

We have a strong privacy law that has had a major effect on information research in Italy. It's a new and hot topic. A recent law has established strict regulations on how one can collect, store, and distribute personal data. The phrase "personal data" refers to all information that can be associated with a person, company, or organization, and is not limited to "sensitive" topics like health or religion. However, information from sources openly available to the public, like print publications, is not considered personal.

The privacy law states that personal data can only be collected with the *written* consent of the subject. It further requires that any collection of personal data, whether digital or print, be reported to a governmental body called Garante. Before personal information can be transferred to a non-European country, the Garante must be informed. As an information researcher working with foreign clients, I have to be careful that the business information I provide would not be characterized as personal, but comes only from sources available to the public.

I sense that the privacy law is impeding our ability to obtain nonpersonal information. Knowing that there's a strong privacy law, people are afraid to give out *any* information, perhaps because they don't understand the law or they misinterpret it, or maybe they just take advantage of the privacy law to withhold information. That's always the reason given why they can't give information. Even when I ask for a document or a piece of information that's not personal, the privacy law is sometimes cited as a reason not to give out information.

Another issue regards the "right to know." This right in Italy is different from that in the United States. In Italy, we have a law informally called the "transparent government" law. A citizen can request a copy of any public document not covered by national secrecy. However, the process by which the public administration must respond is slow and difficult; you have to make a written request that explains your reason for needing to read or copy a public document. The request is evaluated by the administrator of the office that holds the desired information. Important determinants in this decision process are the legal relevance of the request and, of course, the privacy of the people and companies mentioned in the desired document. The public administration has thirty days in which to decide on a request for information, but they only have to respond if the outcome is positive. If they decide not to give out the information, they don't have to respond. So no news is bad news.

In the case of a refusal or no response, the citizen has few alternatives for obtaining the information, although one may try to have the decision reversed by a judge. That's why networking, and getting the same material from alternate sources, are essential strategies.

In my experience, most requests for public documents have been turned down. Rather, I didn't get a response. I've sent a number of requests and only once got a partial, but useful, response. So the problem that I see with the law is that, if you represent a big company or a government agency, you probably will get the information that you want, but if you're a private person or a small company, they may have no reason to give you the information and there's really not much you can do. The law's requirement for a legally relevant motivation may exclude certain requests for information research purposes, especially when the final client wishes to remain confidential. It is not always true that private market research is a legally relevant reason to obtain public information.

Finally, a new Italian copyright law was passed last year, with the particular goal of eliminating the "industry" of illegal reproduction of software and music. However, the law also imposed new regulations for photocopying printed matter. The law requires that libraries and copy centers that permit photocopying pay a copyright fee. The fee is to be collected from the library's users and paid to SIAE, an association that represents authors and publishers. The actual implementation of this law is still to be dictated, and there are ongoing talks between SIAE and several groups representing universities and public or private libraries. The outcome of these talks will be a decision on how libraries should manage the collection and transfer of copyright fees, most likely through a default payment based on size or user base.

Do you encounter any cultural blind spots when you deal with non-Italian clients who are asking for information about Italy?

Yes, in two different ways. People usually ask for the types of information they are accustomed to finding in their own country, and sometimes this information is not available here. I think of cultural blind spots more as a challenge and an opportunity to learn about potential information sources that can be developed in Italy. We don't have a periodical that catalogs the new online resources or that charts the Italian information industry, so I think it's great when I get unusual requests. I have the chance to look for new information sources.

There are also cultural problems in terms of understanding information—how people interpret information, rather than whether they expect it to be available or not. Information has to be interpreted in the appropriate cultural, economic, and political contexts. Despite the many similarities among Western countries, there are subtle differences that should be considered in any analysis. For example, between two countries there may be major differences in university training, access to venture capital, costs of transportation, etc. Therefore, a foreign client who requests information about Italy—to find experts with a certain background or expertise, to evaluate a start-up company, to analyze patterns of retail distribution—must interpret it against the Italian cultural backdrop.

How do you know when you've done a thorough search? How do you know when to stop?

My clients are often researchers or management consultants, so they have a deadline for their information. They might have two weeks, and they need everything then because they have a meeting with their client. Since my research is part of a larger project, we have to pull all the information together by a certain deadline.

A research project can also be terminated when all the relevant sources have been tried. In Italy, the number of databases and other official sources of information is reasonably limited, compared to the U.S. For example, I have found about 150 databases in Italy compared to the ten thousand or so in the U.S. So, if the parameters of the research are well defined, I have just a few sources to check, and then I'm done. For example, if I have to search in Italian newspapers, only a few newspapers make their digital archives available to the public. When the research is on the Internet, it's the deadline and budget of the client that determine how much time I spend.

How do you stay updated on new information sources?

I read the major Italian financial-economic newspaper *Il Sole 24 Ore* [124], which has a weekly section called "The New Economy" dedicated to technology, informatics, and the Internet. I also read an Italian magazine called *Internet News* [189] that has a little bit of everything about the Internet and informatics, both locally in Italy and internationally. The magazine addresses the Internet user rather than the professional searcher. I read other magazines on different topics in Italy, just to get an idea of current trends, especially since there is no periodical that focuses on the Italian information industry. Many magazines now have information about Web sites or other information resources relative to their topic, although their selection may not be appropriate for professional use. Among English-language publications, I read *EContent*, *Searcher* [196] and various science and medical journals to keep up with biomedical issues, the other focus of information research at Up To i.t.

I wind up doing a lot of browsing. We subscribe to many more periodicals than we could ever read. I read the major periodicals and *Il Sole 24 Ore*. The other periodicals are just here to take the place of databases, which we lack. We're developing a specialty library so that, if we need to do manual research through some of these magazines, we can do it. It's an investment. We don't have a great local library where we can go to find all these journals, so we subscribe to the ones that we think are of high quality.

Actually, that ties in with another aspect of my company, which is promoting the use of biomedical literature. It's not just providing access to the literature and not just doing research, but helping people read it, write it, understand it, get closer to it, and understand how the Internet has completely changed access to biomedical literature. So we have a small library of bio-medical journals as well.

What Italy-specific search engines do you rely on when you're doing research?

There is the Yahoo!-like Web catalog called Virgilio, which is useful for finding the URL for a company or a periodical online, or for just doing a quick look-up of something. Virgilio has lists of associations, for example, so I browse through it to find out what's new, and I look there to find new databases. In terms of searching, I prefer AltaVista's advanced search interface, where I can restrict the language to Italian and write a complex string in the large text box. That's where I find the pointers to obscure Web pages. Recently, Google has been giving me better results, with more total hits and fewer dead links, although, compared to AltaVista, the advanced search interface is less flexible. I actually did an informal comparison of Italian search engines with AltaVista, Google and Lycos [89], using a set of ten complex technical queries. I found that Arianna [8] gave a good number of total results—although less than Google—but had comparably high specificity and only about 10 percent dead links.

Besides search engines, what Web-based sources could you not do without?

In terms of free or low-cost sources, I would say that the online catalogs of the books in the Italian library system, Servizio Bibliotecario Nazionale [117], produced by the Istituto Centrale per il Catalogo Unico (ICCU), is a great resource. This unified catalog represents most Italian libraries—academic, public, and institutional—and is useful for searching for books and finding the library in which they are located. Similarly, there is a catalog of periodicals in Italian libraries, called Archivio Collettivo Nazionale dei Periodici [7]. The ICCU also has an ongoing project to develop a document supply center involving all the libraries in the unified catalog; the project is in the experimental stage, but when it becomes active, it should be another step ahead for obtaining information in Italy.

For quick company look-ups, one free resource is the Italian Yellow Pages, called Pagine Gialle [108]. It has three million companies signed up, which is 60 percent of all Italian companies, so it has been a useful, but not comprehensive, resource. Recently, Infoimprese [69], the complete database of the Italian Chambers of Commerce, which is the official Italian company register, has been made available for free on the Web. Infoimprese is produced by a consortium of Italian Chambers of Commerce called InfoCamere [68], and is part of a project called the European Business Registry. As a result of EBR efforts, various European countries have published their company registries on the Web, for free, and often in English as well as in the national language. In Italy's Infoimprese, all of the five million Italian companies are present with their basic registration data. Additionally, companies are able to personalize their entries, and to include information on products, trademarks, Web links, etc.

I think Infoimprese will have a big impact on information research in Italy. What's novel about this site is that it's complete and it's free. Up until now, company directories were either free but not complete, with few details for each company, or they were commercial products like the Dun & Bradstreet [36] database, which has a lot of information on selected larger Italian companies, and costs money to use or buy. Since 98 percent of Italian companies have fewer than twenty employees, the professional databases have not always been useful for generating lists of companies active in a particular sector. Dun & Bradstreet has 500,000 Italian companies, for example, but there are five million companies in Italy. So this new InfoCamere database is going to have real impact, especially because it's free and complete. It's going to encourage people to access public information, I believe.

The free Infoimprese database is possible because companies are obliged to register with the Chambers of Commerce and pay an annual fee. Additionally, the Chambers of Commerce sell access to their data and offer search services on the databases created by InfoCamere. Until the launch of the Infoimprese database, one had to purchase an official document called "visura" just to obtain the general registration information on a company—now this information is available for free on the Web. However, the free database, Infoimprese, only provides basic information, and only permits very simple searches. If you need a financial balance sheet or a list of property holdings, or if you need to use a complex search string, you have to subscribe to the databases of InfoCamere.

So InfoCamere also has a fee-based online service? Tell me more about that. And what fee-based services do you rely on?

There are two sets of essential databases in Italy. The first is the package of InfoCamere databases I mentioned. These are available for subscription through various distributors, not through InfoCamere itself. The distributor I use is Cerved [25]. Cerved also produces some value-added products. They process the information, repackage it, and add some of their own data or that of other public agencies. For example, they have collected information from four different sources about business owners and shareholders of Italian companies, and made a database in which you can search by a person's name and find aggregated information on this person's participation in various companies.

The second essential set of databases is that produced by the group Il Sole 24 Ore, the publisher of the newspaper by the same name. Il Sole 24 Ore also produces various periodicals and online services, one of which is its aggregated database of newspaper and periodical archives. The archives are searchable with a search interface that is useful, reasonably priced and easy to use. There are few other online packages of aggregated databases in Italy. About 80 percent of the 150 databases I have cataloged are sold or published online as single products, directly by the producer.

Since most of the Italian periodicals aren't available online, how do you get copies of articles you need?

Document delivery services don't really exist yet in Italy, but the Italian library system has a document delivery project in an experimental stage. What I do now is network, which works well. It's the old way of getting information in Italy, asking around through people you know. When I need an obscure document, I talk to people I know who are professionals, maybe an accountant or an insurance agent, and they're more than happy to help. They call around, and they end up making appointments for me with some expert in the field. I've also had documents and books mysteriously arrive. Through networking, people are extremely willing to help. Having an introduction through a common acquaintance, even a remote connection, is extremely useful. It's a slow process and it takes a lot of patience. That's the old, traditional way of doing information research.

I balance my techniques. I use the Internet to find unlikely information sources, and I balance that with networking through people I know, so that the documents arrive when I need them. Or I find people who may have the documents in their personal libraries. That's why research takes more time here than in other countries.

How do you think online research is going to change in the next few years?

There has already been a great increase in what's available online and through professional databases. I think that's going to continue; there's no reason it shouldn't. With the growing number of competing products—some free, others fee-based and all with different search features—there's also going to be increasing confusion about where information is to be found, how it can be extracted from the databases, and what value it has. That means that there will be an increasing need for people who are able to find and interpret information, to establish standards, to understand the information, and to catalog what's available. There will be a demand for assistance in sorting it out.

I think that the internal market for information and research services in Italy will grow gradually, due to cultural differences in using information. Right now, people do want information, but they may limit their definition of "information" to finance and credit. They don't appreciate the whole gamut of information and documentation available. They may not believe that reading a selection of periodical literature, newspaper articles, or market research reports can help them make a better decision. Increasing appreciation of information and developing the internal market for research services are gradual processes.

Additionally, since many Italian companies work in Eastern Europe and other opening markets, they may justifiably be hesitant to base their decisions on printed matter of questionable value. And while in Italy the media has been slow to discuss the social or economic importance of information, particularly online information, this may finally be changing. The European Union has recently initiated a program called E-Content, in which they provide financial support for initiatives to increase the awareness of, and access to, public sector information. I believe that the E-Content program will be successful in creating a greater demand for research services as well.

Super Searcher Power Tips

➤ The biggest challenge is that so much information is not available online. I use the Internet to get a bearing on a topic, to understand the issues, to find names of experts or associations, but then I have to follow them up with telephone contacts in order to identify a useful document.

➤ I've really had some successes with AltaVista, writing specific search strings and finding obscure Web sites where information has been posted.

➤ I use the Internet to find unlikely information sources and I balance that with networking through people I know, so that the documents arrive when I need them. Or I find people who may have the documents in their personal libraries.

➤ Networking is the old way of getting information in Italy—asking around through people you know.

Sheri Lanza

From Embassies to Entrepreneurship

Sheri Lanza is the owner of Global Info-Resources, Inc. of Vienna, Virginia, and author of the book, *International Business Information on the Web* (CyberAge Books, 2001). Her company focuses on providing information research and consulting services to clients doing business in the global economy.

lanza@globalinforesources.com
www.globalinforesources.com

Tell me a little about your background and how you got started in your business.

I have a bachelor's degree in math from Miami University in Oxford, Ohio, and an MBA in Finance and Marketing from the University of Miami in Coral Gables, Florida. I started working with computers in the early seventies, in the horrible days of key-punch cards, and I swore I'd never work with computers again. But thirty years later, I'm spending my days glued to the computer.

I've held a number of jobs over the years—I've been a market research analyst for a large medical supply company, I was director of market research and new product development for a cruise line, and I was a financial analyst and a software troubleshooter for a pension valuation firm. I did a stint as a re-engineering consultant for an office at the U.S. Embassy in Costa Rica. This was before there was even a term like "re-engineering," so it wasn't until a few years later that I actually knew that's what I had done. I also worked as the Commercial Attaché at the U.S. Embassy in Costa Rica, and as a research consultant for a firm specializing in mergers and acquisitions. It was after the research job that I started my own business, Global InfoResources Inc., back in 1996. It was just a fluke; I'd never heard of the concept of an independent research business before, but once I started reading about it, I knew I'd finally found what I wanted to be when I grew up.

My husband is in the Foreign Service, which is why we spent eight years overseas—four years in the Dominican Republic and four years in Costa Rica. That is where my international experience and focus began. Now I'd say that about 50 percent of my work is internationally oriented. Most of my clients are U.S. companies that are looking at situations overseas, getting into a business abroad, finding out what the business or economic climate is like in a particular country, or evaluating whether they should pack up and leave a country. So, my research is mostly from the perspective of the U.S. looking out.

Can you describe a typical global research project?

I have a client who works in the defense area, and one of the things they've had me do is look at what sorts of defense or intelligence systems and equipment are being sold to various countries, or what those countries are exporting, what companies in the U.S. might have ties to that country, and those types of things.

So how do I tackle this? First, I make sure I understand the country, and since my client knows quite a bit about the country, I can get a good briefing from them. Then I start with some of the traditional online sources, Dialog [33, see Appendix] and Dow Jones Interactive [35]. This client likes LexisNexis [88] a lot, so I'll check there too. And I have an enormous set of international bookmarks for Web sites, including a lot of directory sites. Since these tend to be very specific types of resources, I make sure that

I've gotten very specific search terms from the client ahead of time, so I know where I'm going. One thing usually leads to another, and either it all leads to a dead end, or it just turns out fabulously and there's a ton of information. It's generally an all-or-nothing proposition. I almost never come back to them with just a little of this, a little of that.

And do you take any other steps if you just don't turn up anything?

I'll check with the client, because sometimes they've got some ideas from prior experience as to where to find things, or suggestions for places that I hadn't thought about. But eventually, it's time to get back to them and tell them that I've looked under all the rocks and looked in all the right places, and this is as far as it's going.

The other thing I sometimes do, once I've done everything I think is appropriate and I'm still not satisfied, is call a colleague for a reality check—kind of like using the phone-a-friend lifeline on *Who Wants to be a Millionaire?* I do that because I need to step back and get some perspective. You know, you get lost in what you're doing sometimes, and you need to talk to somebody else who's knowledgeable but outside the project. I'll say, "Okay, here's what I've done and here's where I've gone. Is there any glaring omission? Is there something you know about that I either forgot or didn't know?"

It's very helpful, because sometimes you want to hit yourself upside the head when you realize an unintentional oversight. As soon as you get the words out of your mouth to somebody else, you think, "Oh my God, I forgot about ..." or "Why didn't I think of ..." Talking it out is a good exercise. Sometimes a little light bulb goes on, and then you can go and do more research. And sometimes you realize, "Gee, I really *have* looked everywhere possible."

Do you have any general rules or tips for searchers doing international research?

First, remember that you can't just rely on the traditional online services anymore, but don't think you can get by just using the Internet either. I've seen a lot of people who think they can do thorough international research for a client just by doing a Web search. They're not fooling anybody except themselves.

But, having said that, I'd still recommend bookmarking several international directory sites and using them for every international project in conjunction with the fee-based services. That's so important.

People also tend to undervalue information from the U.S. government. They often base that on a bad experience they had with some clerk on the phone who didn't have a clue. The U.S. government has a number of great resources for global information. You can try the Department of Commerce [143], Department of State [145], Department of Energy [144], Agency for International Development [140]—all of those can get you started. I also like to use the Web Center on Dow Jones Interactive to get ideas. Often it lists sites that I either hadn't thought of or had forgotten about, so it's helpful to do a quick search through there and see what turns up. And I always check the Chambers of Commerce, foreign embassies, international bank sites, and foreign stock exchanges if I'm doing financial or economic research.

My other advice is not to be afraid to use international search engines. And the most important thing is to stay culturally sensitive and keep your expectations reasonable, so that neither you nor the client is disappointed in the end.

I assume that you speak English and Spanish. What do you do when you're looking for information in other areas of the globe where the information is in another language?

If it's necessary to use sources in a language I can't read, I try to use translation software like Web Translator [206] or Power Translator [205]. Power Translator was originally from GlobalLink, but has been bought by Lernout & Hauspie. They're big in translation; normally they do bigger-scale software rather than tools designed for individuals. They also have human translators. But even when using a translation tool, I look at the translation that I get back much as I would look at an abstract of an article. An abstract lets you know whether or not the article's worth obtaining in full text, although it's no substitute for the actual text. Software-translated text generally tells me whether it's worth obtaining a human translation of the article, whether it looks like it's going in the right direction.

If I really think language is going to be a big hurdle in the project, I prefer to either subcontract the project to someone with the necessary language skills or turn it over completely to someone else. When it makes sense, I set up an arrangement in which I do the portion that involves research in English and have the other person handle the foreign language side. I don't want to take a chance on doing the client a disservice because of my language limitations, and I don't want to provide the client with faulty or inaccurate information because the machine translation wasn't good enough.

Do you find that machine translation works when you're looking through a Web site in a language you don't speak?

The Web Translator software is very helpful, because the results it brings up look exactly like the original Web page—except that the text is now in English—and all your links are still live. That's how I handle foreign language Web sites. But if the text on the page is embedded in a graphic image, translation software won't work because it doesn't recognize the image as text.

If it's in a language that's closely enough related to Spanish—sometimes French, sometimes Italian—even though I can't read it, I can often get enough of a sense of the categories on the page to know whether it's going to be useful.

How have you seen the field of international research change over the past few years?

One of the biggest changes has been the increased importance of the Internet to international research. It's helping reduce some of the roadblocks that existed before due to time differences and language barriers. It is very difficult to call somebody who is eight time zones away, and you still have to deal with the language problem.

Of course, the Internet has also, rightly or wrongly, raised the expectations of our clients. Many of them assume that everyone is out there rushing to make all their information available on the Internet, and that all of it is in English, of course.

The other big change is that the traditional online vendors have made major strides in two areas in the last few years: they've increased the amount of their international content and coverage in English, and they've increased their non-English sources as well. Dow Jones Interactive in particular has made a concerted effort to focus on the international side now, although not to the detriment of the domestic side, obviously. They're really trying to build their international content.

What do you think are the biggest challenges in conducting global research?

Managing the client's expectations while you conduct the reference interview. Not only is the reference interview crucial, as in all types of research, but you need to be a bit more sensitive when you're talking about a global research project. In addition to understanding what information the client needs and why, you need to get a sense of the client's awareness of the culture with which you're going to be dealing. The amount and type of information available can depend on a country's level of economic and social development, its language, religion, and more.

And if the client doesn't even have a cursory understanding of a country or a culture, her expectations can be totally out of line. I know I'm not an expert on all cultures, but I do try to gently educate them about the area in question as best I can so that there are no surprises in the end. For many of my projects, it's particularly important, as they often deal with underdeveloped countries.

I can think of one example where managing my client's expectations was really important. I had a client who was interested in washing machines in Latin America. She had questions like how many were sold, how many were top-loading versus front-loading, how many had built-in fabric softener dispensers, and how many years did people keep a washing machine before purchasing a new one.

The problem was that, given that most Latin American countries are considered developing countries, the project was doomed from the start. By and large, the only people in Latin America who own washing machines are the very wealthy, and that's a small percentage of the population. And a good portion of that group is probably importing washing machines directly from the U.S. instead of buying them on the local market. On top of that, the rest of the people who own washing machines are probably buying them second-, third-, or fourth-hand and they don't care if it's top-loading or front-loading, whether it has a fabric softener dispenser, or whatever. They're just thrilled that they can find a washing machine that they can afford, and that they've got the electricity to use it. So the likelihood of any market research existing on this topic was slim to none, as was the likelihood of finding any relevant articles.

So how did you handle this question? Was the answer "the information doesn't exist?"

Well, prior to starting, I tried to discuss it diplomatically with the client. Luckily, since Latin America was an area in which I had lived, I could speak with some authority and the client knew

I wasn't just talking through my hat. I wanted to be certain that she wasn't expecting full-blown market studies on the trends in washing machine purchases in Latin America. She, of course, had thought it was a very straightforward project, that there would be easily quantifiable results, which there weren't. So, in the end, when very little turned up, she had been prepared for it and it was no big surprise. Obviously, she would have liked to have found the information, but by that point she understood that it wasn't going to be there.

I try to help my clients set reasonable expectations from the beginning, and make them understand that the situations are different in other countries; they can't have the same expectations for the same kinds of results as we would get for the U.S. International research is one of those situations where it's best to underpromise and—one hopes—overdeliver.

If there aren't any regulations requiring the disclosure of particular information, then the information probably isn't going to be available. My best clients are the ones who understand that. When they call me, they'll say, "See if you can find anything about ..." They don't automatically assume that it's going to be there. They're more sensitive to this issue. If nothing turns up or the information is just not obtainable, they understand.

One technique I use, particularly if I'm looking for information on individuals or companies and having trouble finding anything, is to get in touch with the U.S. embassy in that country. I'll talk to someone in the Commercial Section—they have a service available in most countries where, for a nominal amount of money, they will go out and collect the information for you and compile a customized report on the company or individual. It's sort of like a Dun & Bradstreet report, on demand! And if they can't come up with anything, I know that I'm not going to be able to find it. There are only so many rocks you can look under, and if a country's not willing to make the information available, you can't just make it materialize.

Do you have any standard tools that you use to get a quick picture of a country's business etiquette or culture, so that if you're researching in a region that you're not familiar with, you don't wind up committing a faux pas?

Oh yes, there are a number of sources I use. For one, if it's a country that I really don't know anything about, I like to start by reading the overview in the *CIA World Factbook* [26]. Also, I see if there's an American Chamber of Commerce in that country; often a section of its Web site talks about business etiquette or appropriate and inappropriate behavior. All the AmChams—the American Chambers of Commerce overseas—are listed at the U.S. Chamber of Commerce site [141].

Which international search engines do you like?

It depends on the country, but I like Steve Arnold's site [9] as a starting point. It has a section on international search engines. Instead of bookmarking every single site that I like to use, which can get overwhelming, I prefer to bookmark his site, and then scroll through that if I need information on a particular country. Otherwise, I'd have a hundred different search engines book-marked. My bookmarks can get so out of hand; that's why I like directory sites like Steve's so much.

What other resources do you think of as indispensable for global research?

My other favorite is Stat-USA [127]. The Country Commercial Guides can be very good, because they're written from the stand-point of what about this country is good for U.S. businesses, where should they invest. I also find the Industry Sector Analysis reports very useful. I also like the U.S. International Trade Administration's Web site [146]. And there's Statistical Data

Locators [126], from the Nanyang Technological University Library in Singapore.

Another resource I use is from the University of Strathclyde, in Glasgow; it's called Business Information Sources on the Internet [21]. It includes various directory sites, some for international market research, some for trade. There is a problem with updating; some sections are updated more frequently than others. Sometimes I look at the site and see that one section might not have been updated in a year, but then I'll go to another section and find that it was updated three days before. I don't really mind the inconsistency so much with a site like this, because it's more of a directory than a source of the ultimate information. Even if a page hasn't been updated for a year, it's very possible that the site I go to from there was updated that day.

Another site that I think of as indispensable is International Business Resources on the WWW [73], from Michigan State University's Center for International Business Education and Research.

To cover the financial side, there's the Qualisteam Banking and Finance [113] site. Depending on your project, you might also want to check the World Bank [153], the International Monetary Fund [75], regional development banks [114], and embassy sites. And finally, there's the U.S. Chamber of Commerce International Division.

Obviously, you can't do all your research with just these sites, but these are the "don't leave home without them" sites. To shamelessly plug myself here, all of this is summed up in a neat and tidy package in my new book, *International Business Information on the Web* [185]. As the title says, it's just Web sites, both free and pay-as-you-go. Its genesis was the series of articles I did for *Searcher* magazine [196], which was expanded to become a book.

That sounds like a must-have book. Speaking of must-haves, what fee-based online services

would you consider essential for international research?

I couldn't do without at least Dialog and Dow Jones Interactive. Dialog has great databases, depending on what you're looking for. They've got the usual business databases, plus several international company directories, the Global News OneSearch category, regional and country news files, the EIU [37] all in one easy place, and the PIERS [110] databases.

There's also DataStar [31], which I feel you still need to look at, even though some of the international databases are also on Dialog. There are resources on Dialog that aren't on DataStar and vice versa. You need to do a comparison and check each time you start a project. Dow Jones Interactive is great because you can easily focus by country or region, and since it's more business- and news-oriented, it automatically weeds out a lot of extraneous stuff.

I also like to do a quick run through Data Downlink's .xls [159]. I find that it's a good companion resource. The searching is free, it's easy to pick and choose the right databases, and sometimes, looking through the search results, I get inspiration for where else to go.

I have one client for whom I always use Nexis because of the nature of their projects, but I find it easier to get at most of the international information with Dialog and Dow Jones.

If money weren't an object, my wish list would include some of the products from Bureau van Dijk [19], like Amadeus [6] or Fame, which are databases with detailed financial information on European, Irish, and British companies. Unfortunately, since I'm a one-person business, they're out of my reach. But if a client has a subscription, I love to use them.

Do you subscribe to any fee-based online services that are country-specific?

I haven't done that much. Part of the reason is that they tend to be only in the native language, and they're not particularly user-friendly for people who are not native-language speakers. If the need arises to use one of those services, to be fair to the client and to myself I would prefer to contact somebody in that country. I'll probably pull out the membership directory of the Association of Independent Information Professionals [208] and see if we have any members who live in or near that country who might have a better handle on it than I do.

It's a lot harder to know about country-specific databases if you're not in that country or region. For example, if I have to conduct research on something in Italy, I will try to find a colleague in Italy and ask, "Hey, are there any local sources that I don't know about, that I might not even have access to?" As it turns out, some of the sources that they have in Italy just aren't available outside the country. If you want to tap into them, you'd have to use somebody there. I'll only learn that if I deal with somebody who's on the ground in that country.

Where do you think global research is going in the next couple of years?

In many ways it's going to get harder. We're going to be asked to find more information on emerging markets, where there's not as much information available as there is on the more established markets and regions. Those countries are still developing; they need to concentrate on feeding and educating people and keeping infant mortality down, rather than worrying about what they're going to put up on the Web.

By the same token, information about the industrialized countries will not be in as much demand, since clients and users are getting more savvy at searching on their own, and there is so much information available on those countries. The big thing is going to be the emerging markets all over the world—Central and Eastern Europe, the Asian countries, some of the Latin American countries. Africa will be the last market, because there are so many poor countries that just aren't the focus of most global market efforts. We'll stop getting as many projects about, say, what's going on in England. We'll start getting questions on

Croatia and Somalia. What's frustrating is that the sources are more limited there, even on the traditional online services.

Do you think you will see a change in the proportion of primary research that you'll be doing, as opposed to online work?

We may be talking to people a bit more, especially as phone systems overseas improve. And English is becoming more of a global language than it was; now, we're finding people who speak English in even the tiniest, most underdeveloped countries. In terms of print resources, we're not going to see a growth of resources in the emerging market areas. The information's not going to be published quickly in print, and even if it is, it's not going to be updated very often. I think the current information is still going to wind up online, whether it's on the Internet or on Dialog, Dow Jones Interactive, or wherever.

Super Searcher Power Tips

➤ You can't just rely on the traditional online services anymore, but don't think you can get by just using the Internet either.

➤ People tend to undervalue information from the U.S. government, which has a number of great resources for global information.

➤ I'll talk to someone in the Commercial Section of the U.S. embassy in the country I'm researching. They have a service available in most countries where, for a nominal fee, they will collect the information for you and compile a customized report on the company or individual.

➤ Stay culturally sensitive and keep your expectations reasonable, so that neither you nor the client is disappointed in the end.

Wes Edens

International Management Resource Specialist

Wes Edens is the Electronic Resources Librarian at the International Business Information Centre at Thunderbird, The American Graduate School of International Management in Glendale, Arizona. In addition to his reference and research responsibilities, he oversees contracts with database vendors and manages Global Gateway, a Web-based database of sites relating to international business, language, and culture.

edensw@t-bird.edu
www.t-bird.edu/ibic/links

What is your background? What brought you to Thunderbird?

I received a BS in general business in 1987 from the University of Arizona, and for a few years I couldn't figure out what to do with it. This was a time when colleges were turning out undergraduate business majors like me in droves, and the best thing I could hope for was to get some kind of an entry-level management job at a drugstore or convenience store. One day I picked up an old, battered paperback in a used book store; it had been written in the early '70s for men returning from Vietnam, and the title was something like *Nontraditional Careers for Men*. It suggested, among other things, librarianship.

On top of that, my grandmother is a retired librarian, and I always admired her for her choice of careers; it always seemed so noble. By the time I saw the book, I had a personal computer and a subscription to Prodigy, so I fancied myself an amateur researcher. I was kind of surprised to find out I could get an MLS in two years, and that it didn't require any special undergraduate degree. So I started the process of getting into library school. It wasn't until I was almost ready to graduate with my MLS that I realized I could use use my business undergraduate degree to specialize.

So in 1994, I got my MLS from the University of Arizona, and I wound up as the business librarian at the University of North Dakota. I really enjoyed it there, and I had a chance to hone my business skills, but after going through the blizzards and a catastrophic flood in 1997, when my basement turned into a swimming pool, Arizona started to sound pretty good again. I was somewhat familiar with Thunderbird, and I knew that it was highly rated, although not very well known. So when I saw a job opening there, I jumped at it.

Can you tell me a little more about Thunderbird?

We have one campus where I work, here in Glendale, and two overseas centers, one in French Geneva and one in Tokyo. We also have summer programs in Guadalajara, and "winterim" sessions between semesters that involve "learning vacations" in locations all over the world. For example, the environmental policy class might go to Kenya to learn about the environment there. At any given time, about 25 percent of our users are outside the U.S. The library, which we call the International Business Information Centre or IBIC, serves the students throughout the world. We have a small library at the Geneva center but it's very basic. They rely on our virtual library on the Web. The Internet has really been a boon. Because of the time differences, the non-U.S. students aren't taxing the resources at the same time the U.S. students are using them.

The staff of the IBIC give presentations to executives who come in from all over the world. We did one for Ericsson recently on secondary market research and competitive intelligence, for example. Thunderbird is really focused on the international aspect of business. Up until now, the School has offered a Master of International Management degree. Whether we will spread into the more traditional MBA market remains to be seen. Despite the fact that we haven't been offering an MBA, we're ranked against the top schools that do. And Thunderbird has been ranked the top MBA program for international business by *U.S. News and World Report* for six years in a row.

We also have a fee-based service, called Business Information Service [20, see Appendix]. We have global clients, mostly alumni, but it's open to anybody. The BIS uses the IBIC reference collection and the databases for which we have information intermediary licenses. Much of what we do involves questions like the market size of an industry, or background on a specific product in a particular region. We have two staff members who work primarily on BIS, and they farm some of the work out to the rest of us on the staff. Information on BIS pricing and some sample questions are at the BIS Web site.

What is a typical global research question that you get in the IBIC?

We get a lot of questions along the lines of "What is the market for bottled water in Argentina?" or "How many mountain bikes were sold in Chile last year?" or "I need to know about the boat-building industry in Mexico." For these types of questions, we use Business Reference Suite [22], primarily because of the way it's indexed. It's indexed in depth and it uses terms that our researchers would use. We are also really heavy users of Stat-USA [127]. We use the Country Commercial Guides and the Industry Sector Analyses quite a bit. In fact, we have to warn the professors here not to give assignments that are too close to what's in the Industry Sector Analyses, because the students could come in and get all their work done from one ISA report.

We're also one of the largest academic clients in the world for the Economist Intelligence Unit [37] database. It's our most expensive resource and one to which we limit access. Instead of allowing students to log on to it through the network, as they can with most of our other Web-based databases, we can only have it available on kiosks in the IBIC. We also use Euromonitor's Global Market Information Database [56] for the consumer market.

Do you maintain much of a print collection, or do you focus on Internet- and intranet-based resources?

Well, being the database guy here, I'm heavily biased in favor of the electronic resources, so I usually look first at the electronic material when I'm doing research, and then I look at what we have in our print collection. More and more, though, our major print sources are migrating to the Web. Take *Political Risk Yearbook* [194], for example; we now use the Web version instead of print. We were getting all the consumer research books from Euromonitor [42]; now we use the Global Market Information Database. More and more, we're able to answer questions using the Web-based sources. One exception is the International Monetary Fund's *International Financial Statistics* [186]; it is heavily used here in print and on CD-ROM, and we hope to see that on the Web one day.

Do you find that your students from various areas of the world use different techniques for looking for information?

Yes. For example, about one out of every seven Thunderbird students is in our Latin American program and many of them are from Mexico. We find that they're accustomed to not having a lot of databases. They've been used to having information fed to them by teachers and learning by rote memorization. We have to show them that they can do a lot of the research on their own now.

And do *you* have different research techniques for finding information in different regions of the world?

I would say so, especially when I am doing research on Latin America or Japan. A lot of times, I use the Web to find *people* instead of finding information. For instance, I have a friend who's the director of a virtual library for a university in Monterrey, Mexico. If I have a tough question about Latin American business, I might check with her and ask, "Am I missing something?" The same is true for research on Japan. We have a database produced in Japan, Nikkei Net Interactive [99], that we use for Japanese research, but I would probably use the Web as well to find people who know something about the topic. We have a large alumni network, and about 10,000 of the alumni use our intranet. Although the network hasn't been used extensively so far, it is another way to check with people on the ground in the country you're researching.

What changes have you seen in the resources that are available for Internet research over the last few years?

The Web is slowly starting to become more truly global, especially with the non-Latin character sets that are available now. We have a lot of Asian students, and they used to run around and install shareware that put Asian character fonts on our terminals. Sometimes it worked okay, but sometimes it would cause the machines to crash. It was a problem. Now that Internet Explorer can handle all those different character sets, I think the Web is going to start exploding into some areas that have not been well represented.

Speaking of language, how do you handle doing research in areas in which most of the resources are not in English?

We have a multilingual staff; there are people who speak Portuguese, French, Spanish, German, and a smattering of other languages. Most of the time, the person asking the question is fluent in the language, so he or she just needs some help in getting started. If I have to, I'll translate search terms using an online dictionary like Babelfish [201] in AltaVista, or a print dictionary, and then I'll search using those terms. I can usually read enough Spanish to figure out if I'm on track. If not, I'll use the Web page translation service with Babelfish. Although it's not perfect, it usually tells me enough to know whether I've found what I'm looking for. Then I'll send the information on to the end-user and find out if that's what he or she needed.

For instance, I had a question from somebody who wanted some demographic information on the Buenos Aires province of Argentina. It had to be from that specific province. She wanted income and housing data, so I used a few terms in English and in Spanish and found an Argentine government Web site that covered just that province. It gave exactly the information she wanted. So sometimes you can answer the question if you know just a little bit of the language.

How do you validate sources that you're not familiar with? I would think that this would be even more of a problem when the site isn't in English.

We do the best we can by looking at who maintains the site, and looking at the domain—is it a government site or an educational site or whatever. Then we apply some of the other criteria that people use for evaluating Web sites. We look at the amount of advertising on the page; we see whether it seems to be biased in favor of a particular political view, if it's trying to sell you something. We look at the objectivity of the site, the content, the timeliness, and whether we can verify the information using other material.

Even when the site is in English, you shouldn't take things at face value. For instance, one of the reasons why people like Stat-USA so much and why it's so highly regarded is because it comes from the U.S. Department of Commerce. But one of our marketing professors insists that you really don't know whether the person whose name is on the report actually wrote the last update, or whether it was updated by a college intern who did some sloppy research and just threw it together. So we always try to triangulate the information from other sources, if possible. And if we can't, we always warn our patron that we're not sure about the reliability of the source, but that this was the only source we could find that had data on the question.

What's the biggest challenge that you run into when you're doing international research?

The hardest thing is that there are assumptions about what's available out there. For instance, Americans tend to think that there will be equivalent resources for the rest of the world to what they use for North American research. Often, they're surprised to learn that there just isn't a good equivalent to, say, *Standard and Poor's Industry Surveys* [197]. Or they're surprised that there's not an equivalent of the U.S. Securities & Exchange Commission's EDGAR [148] files for every country, for free out there on the Web.

There are some parts of the world where it's just hard to get any information. Mexico really stands out in this regard. Sometimes the information just isn't there—or if it is there, it's in a format that we can't reach. It might be in hard copy in a library somewhere in Mexico or somewhere in Russia.

So our two biggest challenges are the assumption that everything's out there, online for free, and the unpleasant fact that, often, the information simply doesn't exist.

We also run into the problem where people are asked to research how to introduce a product into a country where that product isn't in use, and we find that there could be cultural reasons for the fact that there isn't a market for the product. Introducing peanut butter into Poland is a very typical example. As far as we know, the Poles don't eat peanut butter. We help users get over the shock that they're asking a question that is too specific or that's just not appropriate for that region or that culture, and then we try to help them find similar products or similar concepts for that region. If we're doing the peanut butter market, we might help them find out the market size for bread in Poland, or figure out another way to work around the problem and make inferences.

Some of these little-known facts, like peanut butter in Poland, are just part of the library lore that gets passed down from librarian to librarian. And we know that this is part of the game the instructors play to shake up the students a little, so we're prepared for it. We know that those questions are going to come every semester, so when a student comes up with a question about marketing a specific product in a specific country, we're always on guard that this may be a curve ball.

We also have an online reference service that we run on our intranet, called Ask IBIC. Unlike an email reference service, it's a message board, so a lot of students watch the questions and answers. When somebody posts a question there, they have to spell it out in black and white for us, and we can ask follow-up questions. What's nice is that we have a record of these questions that everyone can see. So if someone else gets a similar question, they might be able to say, "I remember that we had to find a Web site that covered the Argentine wine industry last month."

Right now, the questions expire after ninety days, but we're working on building a knowledge-based tool around it. We'd like to build up an Ask Jeeves-type service with these questions and answers, because we do get questions that are just slight variations on ones someone asked six months ago. Of course, sometimes the answer that we find will be dated; we can't rely on work done six months ago, but we'd like to use the same search strategies in the commercial databases. What's hard is that our standard research sources seem to change so frequently; a Web site that was the best source last month may be completely redesigned or will have lost all the useful free information the next time we look at it.

Are there any other factors that really make international research difficult?

Working with vendors can be difficult when you're dealing with international locations. I always assume that the vendors know what I'm talking about when I say "remote access for our users." But a vendor in the U.K. said to me, "Your users can dial in to your host computer and so that's remote access." No—to me, remote access is when they're in Antarctica and they need to have access to our databases.

Another time, the same U.K. vendor cut off one of our subscriptions because they had mixed up the different ways that Americans and Europeans write the dates, MMDDYY or DD-MMYY. That's one of those problems in which each side thinks that this is totally obvious, and neither side realizes that there is a disconnect.

I forget sometimes when I'm searching, even in an English-language source, that I have to be careful with the terms that I use. If I'm searching Euromonitor, for example, I have to remember to say aluminium instead of aluminum, or turnover instead of sales. If I don't, then I won't find anything.

How do you know when you've done a complete search, especially when you're working on a region of the world with which you're not familiar?

After I've searched everything I can think of, I check with my colleagues here, because print resources are a blind spot for me. I also check the IBIC's Global Gateway page [55] to see if anything listed there might be useful. A good example of a Web site that we use to answer a lot of questions is Oanda [101], which is a currency calculator that also gives you daily exchange rates going back decades. It's very useful, and it's free. If the project I'm working on involves a subject that we teach here at Thunderbird, I'll call faculty members and ask them if I'm on the right track, or if they even think this information exists. After I've exhausted those routes, I'll do a final check on the BUSLIB [165] email discussion list. If I don't get anything there, then I'm pretty sure that I've done all I can.

How do you stay updated on new information sources?

I learn a lot by going to conferences, attending as many sessions as I can and visiting the exhibit hall. I read a lot of publications; we route *Business Information Alert* [164], *Information Advisor* [181], *Searcher* [196], *Online* [192], *CyberSkeptic's Guide to Internet Research* [169], *Charleston Advisor* [166], and *EContent* [172] to all the librarians.

One thing that I've learned is that the true power of the Web lies in the community; millions of people are now having conversations about everything under the sun. If you can find an electronic discussion group that covers your topic and can post your question there, like we do with BUSLIB, then you can really tap into the power of the Web. And if you get to know the people who are behind the databases, like Howard Holmes from Kompass USA [83], then you can work with them. They ask you for your input or advice, and when you have a problem or a request that's a little out of the ordinary, they're more than willing to help out.

Do you use any country-specific Web search engines?

No, although we do include a lot of those search engines in Global Gateway. When I get a question, I usually don't have time to become familiar with a new search engine just for that question, so I rely heavily on two search engines—Google [59] and AltaVista [4].

What free or low-cost Web-based sources do you rely on?

We use Stat-USA a lot, as I mentioned already, and Kompass. Ideally, we would like to have Dun & Bradstreet's [36] worldwide company database, but it's just not available for academic libraries. So we rely on Kompass. It's not perfect, since it doesn't include Japan or much of Latin America. But for the countries it does cover, it's very impressive, and it's inexpensive.

We also use a lot of the U.S. government sites, like the International Trade Commission [147]. We use U.S. government sites here quite a bit for import/export-type questions. We also look for the U.S. Chamber of Commerce [141]—Am Chams—to see if they have a directory of members, although most of the time I find that the directory is not on the Web.

As for the print sources that I consult regularly, I often use the World Bank's *Global Development Finance* [179]. We also have a lot of encyclopedias, and we rely on government sources that produce statistical abstracts in print as well as on the Web, like Statistics Canada [128]. We use the *Political Risk Yearbook* [194], both online and print, quite a bit. We're often asked to come up with lists of U.S. companies operating abroad, and the best source for this still seems to be a print source, *Directory of American Firms Operating in Foreign Countries* [171].

Which professional or high-end online services do you find the most useful?

We use the Economist Intelligence Unit quite a bit. And we use Business Reference Suite to answer probably half of our reference questions. It's the first place we check for a lot of questions. We also use Euromonitor's Global Market Information Database and sources from the International Monetary Fund [75]. And we use ISI Emerging Markets [78] when we need information that's hard to get elsewhere. For instance, I had a group of students who were looking for information on the Indian economy, so they decided that they needed data from the Centre for Monitoring the Indian Economy [24]. It's really hard to get their material, but the information is in ISI Emerging Markets.

Every emerging-market country is unique; we can't develop a template of information sources that will work for research on every country, since the resources vary so much. We often suggest that students start with the country's central bank. There is a trade-off, though. If you're doing research on several countries and you go to the central bank in each one, you may not have consistent data across the board. On the other hand, if you limit your sources to those that look at multiple countries, you miss the unique sources that one country might offer. Some sources in ISI are common across different countries. So we often rely on a combination of standard and unique sources.

We also have a strong collection of international newspapers, which our students really like. We can't keep the print copies for more than a couple of months, but ISI has the newspapers, in English and in the language of the country, going back several years. And we also just got Dow Jones Interactive [35] for both the School and the Business Information Service, and we use it quite a bit. Its coverage is so broad that we were able to get rid of some of our other databases and just rely on DJI. We use a lot of analyst reports and industry association reports, and for those we turn to Investext [135].

How do you think global research will change in three or four years?

Well, I'm not sure we're going to be doing things differently in three years. Bill Gates once said that people tend to overestimate the amount of change that's going to happen in five years, but dramatically underestimate the amount of change that will happen in twenty years. Wireless Web access may affect us if it ever takes off here in the U.S. Our IT people here don't seem to think that it will, but it's possible that people will be accessing our databases using wireless appliances.

I think the Web today is just a pale glimmer of what it's going to be ten years from now. Who would have guessed in 1991 where we would be today? I think e-books are going to have such a tremendous impact; we're already seeing periodicals go digital, and now reference books are shifting to the Web and, at least for business users, it's going to be monographs next. I don't think people are going to want to read novels in an e-book format for quite a while, but maybe they will, depending on how the technology evolves. Now, we're mailing books and videos through the postal service to people all over the world, and I don't think we'll be doing that in ten years. We'll be delivering a lot more information electronically, and making more of our collection available online. Bandwidth is going to continue to increase, so one day we won't even have to mail videos.

I think our international business education will be increasingly scattered across the globe. We're already seeing fewer people come here to the Glendale campus; soon, we'll have a lot more Web-based education. People will be able to do most of their coursework at home in Europe, and then just come here for one semester. We already have our Latin American program where they spend two weeks here, two weeks at a Latin American campus, and then they do the rest via live videoconferencing. Distance learning is going to play a much bigger role.

I think that online databases are going to be increasingly available and affordable. Right now we can't afford the market research firms' databases, for instance, but I'm not sure they can continue to charge the kinds of fees they do now. We've seen Dialog [33] learning the hard way about pricing; who would have imagined, several years ago, that today you could search most of Dialog's content for free, and then pay a few dollars with your credit card for just the article you want, using Dialog's Open Access service?

After we show our students Dow Jones Interactive, they ask us, "How do we get the same resources after we graduate?" I tell them that they can get a subscription to Dow Jones Interactive for $69 a year, and then pay about three bucks for an article. I suggest they combine that with what they can get with a credit card on Dialog. But they don't want to hear that; they want to hear that they can pay $50 a year and have full access to all the information that we provide. But then you look at FT.com [52] and how much you can get for free. It's unbelievable. So I think that the trend toward the democratization of information is going to continue.

Super Searcher Power Tips

➤ Often, I use the Web to find *people* instead of finding information.

➤ Our two biggest challenges are the assumption that everything's out there, online for free, and the fact that often there is nothing available.

➤ To verify quality and reliability, always try to triangulate the information from other sources.

➤ Every emerging market country is unique; we can't develop a template of information sources that will work for research on every country, since the resources vary so much. We often suggest that students start with the country's central bank, especially for macroeconomic questions.

➤ Get to know your vendors. The people behind the databases are often your best allies.

➤ Watch your language. Even if you don't know the language, you may be able to get started with a dictionary and an online Web translator like Babelfish. Even in English, make sure you cover all your bases by using alternative terms, such as "aluminium" as well as "aluminum."

➤ The true power of the Web lies in the community; millions of people are now having conversations about everything under the sun.

Tracey Collinson
Investment Banking Research on the Pacific Rim

Tracey Collinson is the manager of the Business Research Centre at JP Morgan in Hong Kong.

collinson_tracey@jpmorgan.com

First, can you tell me about your background?

I've been working for JP Morgan as a Business Research Centre manager for nine years. I started at JP Morgan as a temporary employee in the Melbourne, Australia, office. I hadn't worked in this field at all, although some of my prior jobs had touched on research. I had a thorough knowledge of company research from working at the Stock Exchange in Australia, as well as in the management consultancy division of Price Waterhouse in Melbourne. Later on, JP Morgan decided to throw away their library because they found they just weren't getting enough use out of it, and they asked me to come in temporarily and just keep things going for a couple of weeks—you know, put a few things away and help toss things out. And I looked around me and thought, "How can these people do what they need to do without any information resources?" I was sort of working in a corner at that point; there wasn't even a PC, just piles and piles of things on the floor.

I started looking at everything and realized that there was a lot of good stuff, but there was also a lot of rubbish. I talked to the bankers and found out what their needs were and what I thought I could do for them. I discovered that, yes, they did have a need for information, but they didn't want a library; what they wanted was a corporate resource centre, which would include things like company documents and brokerage reports, rather than things like time series of economic statistics from the government bureau of statistics going back ten years. I decided that, since it would be just me working there, I wouldn't have time to maintain a big collection of books and other material. So I kept just a small collection of annual reports and broker research reports and a few reference books that were being used quite a lot, and threw the rest away.

This caught the attention of the managing director. Here I was, throwing three-quarters of the library out, and now people were beginning to use the library. So we had a chat and the managing director said, "Well, why don't you talk to people around our network, and we can offer you a job. We don't know quite what it's going to be, but we can find something for you to do, I'm sure." So my job sort of evolved. They sent me on a trip around the world. I went to the Tokyo, New York, and London offices and found out that they had really strong research departments and people were doing very in-depth research. One of the things I had done before leaving on that trip was order Inmagic [204, see Appendix], which I found from looking through a phone directory left by the previous librarian. I talked to the Inmagic people, found out what it could do, and designed a new Inmagic database to keep track of the corporate resources.

I worked in that job for six years. Of course, during that time, with the advent of technology, we went from having an Inmagic database on a stand-alone PC in my little corner to a networked situation with email where we could share information. We moved to Lotus Notes, and we transformed the Inmagic database into Lotus Notes and started putting databases on people's desktops. After I'd been there for six years, they gave me the opportunity to come here to Hong Kong and basically do the whole thing again. They had another library that needed a revamp; again we threw away much of the material.

So the Business Research Centre here in Hong Kong supports the Asia and Australia region, which includes sixteen countries, excluding Japan. Most of the research we do is for investment banking, which includes takeovers, mergers and acquisitions, and that sort of thing. About 80 percent of our business, both here in Asia and generally speaking for the BRCs globally, comes from investment banking clients. However, this will soon change dramatically due to our recent merger with Chase Manhattan, Jardine Fleming, and Ord Minnett—the latter two being strong in equities and asset management, which are areas in which JP Morgan had far less of a presence in Asia.

In the pecking order, there are analysts, then associates, and then senior bankers, vice presidents, and the like. The research support we provide tends to be more at the junior analyst level. The analysts, of course, do a lot of the research work, so they're our main focus. We provide both research support and databases on their desktops, so we also provide training to help them use those databases. A big part of my job is managing the vendor relationships, both locally and within a global context.

Can you describe a typical international research project?

First, keep in mind that the research we do for the senior bankers is a lot different from the types of questions that would be asked by a junior analyst. The senior bankers tend to be in a mad rush for things like current news on a director or someone they are about to meet, or latest-breaking financial results. We often get asked to do analyses of whole markets. For example, we might look at the size of the equity market for IPOs in Asia in the last three years, broken down by industry.

At the more junior level, we usually get more specific, nitty-gritty types of questions. For example, we get requests to do searches on every company in Asia in a given sector, provide share prices and values going back five years, spreadsheets showing any mergers or acquisitions they have been involved in, market research on the sector, that kind of thing.

We tend to get asked fairly straightforward questions, rather than the more meaty research-oriented questions that we used to get. I think that's because people can find a lot of information themselves on the Internet. They know that if they're looking for industry research, for example, they can get on the Internet and look for an industry association's site or use some of the electronic databases that we make accessible on the desktop. They're getting more and more adept at finding those sorts of things themselves.

For that matter, the Internet has changed how we do things here in the BRC as well. Instead of having to spend a lot of time on research requests, we can now focus on training issues, Web site development, and new product evaluation. These sorts of things often used to be put on the back burner, because we were so tied up with handling information requests, but now we're increasingly able to bring them to the front burner.

When you train analysts, do you help them figure out the appropriate Web sites to go to for certain kinds of information, or do you focus on showing them how to use search engines and other finding tools?

When new hires start or when people transfer in from another region, we run an introduction course, which is about two hours long. It covers what kind of information databases are available on the desktop, how to fill out an electronic request form in Lotus Notes, and how to use our catalogue. Internet training is part of that course. Most people know how to do basic Internet research, so they're impatient to move on past that subject. But I show them a few little searching tricks, and I also provide them with a short guide showing the various kinds of search logic and how using that logic can affect the outcome of the search.

Generally speaking, I find that the analysts who are coming straight out of university are pretty good at getting information for themselves.

While people with our background know some things that others don't, it's not very hard to learn how to do Internet research well if you're motivated to learn. When training the analysts, we give them tips that will improve their productivity, and we back that up with things like compiling lists of Web sites that we recommend and posting the lists on an intranet page, and suggesting search engines that we think are better in terms of getting results targeted towards our business outcome.

Each of the BRCs currently has a Web site of its own, and they are accessible through a map of Business Research Centres on the main investment banking intranet site. Each of the BRC sites has a section on Internet infolinks, and we all try to add to it from time to time and improve it as we go along. People really like learning about new sources, because often they just don't have the time to try to embrace the vast scope of information out there on the Internet.

This is why, increasingly, I am focusing on finding Web products which include aggregated lists of sites, pulled together by industry, by region, and by country. The best of these categorise the sites into groupings that use terminology that the analysts would understand— "telecoms and technology," for example, rather than "cable." These are tools the more senior bankers will use also, because they're so pressed for time and in some cases they're not all that Internet-proficient.

Sites like this save people time by helping them find the most valuable information quickly and easily. The whole point is that you can train your clients, but at the end of the day, if you don't also make it easy for them to find things of value, then you're not really doing your job.

How do you stay on top of the new information sources?

The online vendors call or come by when they've got anything new, and I always make myself available for that. Sometimes they float things by me that I take one look at and know that I won't find useful. But other times they have made dramatic improvements to products that previously I wouldn't have considered, so it pays to keep an open mind. I also hear about new sources from reading the information industry magazines and from just talking with people. The bankers here are pretty good at alerting me when they find resources that they think could be useful, and we work in an atmosphere where people are encouraged to exchange that sort of information.

I could spend four times as much time keeping up to date on resources as I spend now. I do go to a conference every year, sometimes in the U.S. and sometimes in Europe; last year I went to the European Business Information Conference [209] in Amsterdam. Conferences always provide good opportunities to spend concentrated time getting up to date on new products and industry developments.

But, to be realistic, we're a small unit and we don't have the luxury of a large research staff. A manager like me spends half the day doing research, and wears so many hats, that finding the time to keep up on what's going on globally is a luxury, although in fact it should be a priority. Currently we are in expansion mode to accommodate the increased demands on us by the integrated JPM Chase group, so I'm hoping I'll be able to spend more time on development issues soon.

How has global research changed in the past couple of years?

There used to be more Asian resources, and over the last few years we have seen them get gobbled up by the larger companies like Thomson and Primark, or seen their information absorbed into other, more global databases. When the markets crashed in Asia in 1997–1998, a lot of smaller information companies didn't survive.

Almost all of the databases that we use here are global databases. There are very few databases specifically designed for Asian research, and that poses a couple of problems. First, companies produce documents or information in their local language, and the big, globally focused databases often don't include that content; it just gets dropped, and you'd never know you're missing it.

The other problem is that a lot of the databases tend to be very U.S.-centric, and their local offices, which are often quite small, have a limited ability to obtain information from their head offices or to make changes in the product in any way. As a result, in some cases the Asian content hasn't been as rigorously checked or frequently updated as the U.S. or European content. Then there are cases where, for example, content is collected in Thailand or one of the other Asian countries, then sent to the Hong Kong office, then sent on to the New York office to be added to the database. The whole process can take quite a lot of time, which means that information is not in the database as quickly as you need it to be.

We have become more reliant on local Web sites and so on, rather than traditional databases, particularly for company information. We will often go directly to a company's Web site to find financial information, for example. The problem with that is that, while the largest companies in the region produce pretty good sites and make their documents available, anything from the middle tier down is very hit or miss. From my perspective as someone who doesn't speak or read Chinese, for example, I'm sure that I'm missing lots of Chinese-language resources. I do have a great senior researcher who is Chinese, so she does a lot of the research that is Chinese-focused, because so much of that information is just not available in English.

On the other hand, we still have problems finding people who can read the specific Asian language that we need to translate. For example, one of the end-users here needed information on a Korean company, and we couldn't find anything in the professional databases. She found some information at the company's

Web site, which was in Korean. But she is Chinese and can't read Korean, so she found someone in the Korea office who could translate enough of it for her to get the basic financial information she needed. Ten points for her perseverance!

At that point, she was told by somebody in the Seoul office about a Korean database that contains company financials, and she asked me if I could find out more about subscribing to it. Well, on doing so, I found out that the site is in Korean and even the Seoul office contract was written in Korean. I looked at it and thought, "There's just no way that we can use this resource!" Sometimes there are resources that we are aware of, but we can't access as we would like to.

Do you encounter problems related to differing laws concerning financial disclosure in various countries?

Yes, although I would say that it's more the case that there isn't enough regulation, and there isn't enough monitoring of information in a lot of the countries. There are two sides of this coin. One is that, for example, if I want to get information on a private company in Asia, the only real source that I have is Dun & Bradstreet [36], or the local regulatory commission. But the local regulatory commission may not be particularly adept at putting in place guidelines and regulations about what information must be submitted and in what format. The information may be there, but it is hit or miss. Then getting access to it is difficult. A lot of times, the commissions don't have Web sites, or if they do, they don't have an English-language version. So I have to rely on local people in our offices in each country to tell me that the resources exist. But I find that, even if I locate the Web site and it is in English, I still often can't get the information, because they haven't done a very good job collecting it. That's been part of the reason why the markets and the economies here crashed as they did so dramatically—so little regulation of companies and financial markets existed in many of those countries three years ago.

Now, they realize that they have to take the role of watchdog more seriously, and obtain and disseminate information from companies and industries more effectively, so that the fiscal crises that happened here don't happen again.

On the other side of the coin, you've got situations like China, where the government just doesn't want people to know too much detail about economic matters. They tend to use favoured press sources like the Xinhua News Agency [158] to communicate information. They'll make announcements about economic statistics or industries, but it's very limited information, and you have no way of checking its accuracy—the news release is all you have.

However, as China opens up more and more, and increasingly allows western companies in, this is beginning to change. For example, there was an interesting development a couple of years ago; the *Financial Times* realized that it didn't have a lot of access to Chinese government announcements and economic information, so it set up a joint venture with the Chinese government whereby it provided people to teach local government employees English and reporting and writing skills, and in return it would get English versions of the Chinese government press releases and economic statements.

When you get a call from a client who wants financial information on a company in a country where corporate information isn't collected very well, what do you do?

You do everything you can, exhaust every avenue that you have, and then you give up! Sometimes you just have to grasp at straws—you try to get bits and pieces here and there. And you try to think laterally when you're searching a database. For example, we do a lot of research on individual components of computers and televisions. So we'll be looking for information on the market for one tiny component that we've never heard of before and may never hear of again, and we're looking for the factories that produce it, and so on. It may be not be manufactured anywhere else in the world, but it may be a major industry sector here in Asia. What you have to do is to start thinking laterally. You think, okay, I can't get anything on this industry specifically, but what about companies that are in similar or related industries globally? Or perhaps the major company in this sector is owned by a U.S. company, so we might look at research on that U.S. company and hope that we'll find a sentence or two about their Korean plant or something like that. We think as broadly as we can in using what resources we have.

Sometimes we can get in contact with industry associations, though often, again, the Web sites or materials they produce are only in the local language. Unfortunately, there isn't a directory specifically of Asian industry associations. We'll also do news searching ad nauseum, to see if we can find a quote or some piece of information attributed to a source, and then follow that up. Sometimes we just have to back into the information by using the traditional global-type resources and then following clues to a local level.

It sounds like you do a lot more detective work than researchers in the U.S. or Europe.

I really think I should just retire and write a detective novel about online searching! The big thing that drives all of these issues is that we're working in investment banking and we don't have the luxury of time; whatever we do is always under a huge time pressure. There's a point where you just have to say, "Okay, I don't have the time to spend chasing up all of the leads, so what's the one lead that looks most likely?" You follow that one up, and if you get to the end of the tunnel and there's just nothing there, you have to accept it and move on, because you just don't have the time to take it to the next step. In some ways, that's frustrating, but in other ways it's quite a relief, because you don't have to spend all that time searching when, in your heart of hearts, you know you're most likely never going to find anything anyway.

What other challenges do you run into when you're doing international research?

Dealing with documents that are in the local language and not in English. That drives me crazy. Being hung up on is the other thing that drives me crazy. If you call a phone number and the person who answers doesn't speak English, he'll just hang up in your face. When you make business phone calls where you're trying to communicate and you're not getting anywhere, eventually it's just easier for one or the other of you to hang up, and that can be very frustrating.

I tend not to make phone calls if I can avoid it. Candice, my senior researcher here, is fluent in Cantonese, so when phone calls need to be made to companies or industry groups in China or Hong Kong, for example, she will make those calls, which is great. Or perhaps I might get someone in the Seoul or the Singapore office to make the phone calls or to follow up. I can't do the sorts of things that I used to do in Australia, where we just had one language, English, and it was the one that I spoke. There, you really pumped the fires and worked your networks and that sort of thing.

When I was Australia, I would learn an awful lot from other information professionals; I was part of an Australian industry group similar to the Special Libraries Association [215]. In fact, the issue of keeping up to date on the industry is a big black hole for me here. There are some very good people in this industry, but they are all locals, so when we do get together for industry meetings, as much as I enjoy meeting people and as much as they try to include me in the conversation, ultimately it all comes back to the fact that they are speaking Cantonese and I'm the only one who can't. So I miss out on the industry network here that I used to be tied into in Australia. But them's the breaks.

What do you find most rewarding about doing international research?

Having moved from Australia—which is such a small place in the global scheme of things, and which in some ways is a bit isolated—and coming up to Asia and doing research on this region, my eyes have been opened to the big wide world. I've learned a lot about political and cultural aspects of the countries up here. Even though Australia is part of the Asia-Pacific region and sees itself in many ways as a member of that community, when you live in a country, you are mainly just aware of your own back yard. Coming up here, doing research on Asian industries, companies, and markets, has given me a much broader view of how this part of the world works as a region. Topics like the electronic components markets, which I would never have even considered needing to know about, all of a sudden I find interesting, whereas in Australia I focused on mining, which I have never once done any research on here. You can identify with the bigger scheme of things, in a global sense, more easily when you have a broader regional view.

From a personal perspective, I've learned a lot about the cultural side of learning, about communicating information, about situations where people might be more reluctant to speak directly, to criticize, or to say what they really think about something. And I feel that my career has broadened, and my own personal level of knowledge has expanded, and I feel good about that. It has triggered an interest in finding out more about other places and other cultures that I wouldn't have been interested in had I stayed in Australia.

Since you have analysts from all over the world, do you often run into cultural blind spots?

Well, it's interesting. JP Morgan people are transferred around a lot. We find that people who come here from other regions—and I suppose this includes me, because I'm not native to Hong Kong, either—bring with them a set of assumptions about what is available, or the level of disclosure required by companies or whatever. When you first move out to Asia, you have to completely change your assumption base, and that can be quite difficult—adjusting to a whole new environment where things aren't so transparent. That is one of the big challenges of working in Asia.

We have situations, for example, where people come here from the analysts' training program in New York and they start asking us to get them a breakdown of share ownership of a particular company. But here in Asia, a lot of the companies are part of family-owned empires, and even when they're public, the ultimate holding company might be a family company that isn't public. So these big conglomerates aren't necessarily going out of their way to disclose their structure or finances. Coming up against that lack of information can be quite frustrating. These issues come up a lot, and you learn patience working here. I can't just log onto a database and get the information that I was accustomed to finding in Australia.

How do you know when you've finished with a project; how do you know if you might be missing an important source?

Sometimes, you'll just run into a wall and you can't get inside a source. For example, recently we were trying to get some information on a private company in Singapore. The regulatory commission there has a Web site that I was able to find, and I made a couple of calls to people who said, "Yes, you can get that sort of information." I looked through the Web site and I looked at third-party suppliers of the same information, but not one of them provided electronic access to the source documents. So, the information was there but I couldn't get at it. The only way anyone could get the information was to queue up with a number and use the commission's microfiche—in Singapore.

So it comes down to a question of how much we need this information, and what time frame we are working in. Should we send one of the assistants from that office out to do this for us; is it worth going to that trouble? We often can't physically go to the source if something isn't available electronically, and that can be frustrating.

I also sense that language differences are getting in the way of finding information. As you spend more time working in different countries, you do get an intuitive feel for whether you're missing something, or whether anything exists at all. And we're often working within very short time frames, so I might think, "I've done 98 percent of what I can, and I could probably get another 2 percent if I had the time, or if I had more resources, or if I knew the language, or if I were in that country. But this is the best I can do." That can be frustrating if you're a perfectionist, as I tend to be. But, you know, 98 percent is a pretty good effort.

What Web-based resources do you consider to be critical for international research, and what do you make available through the BRCs' intranet sites?

The Business Research Centres around the world work very closely together, and we have developed a toolkit of Web-based products which we pump through our various intranet sites. We don't really customise them at this point; rather, we just provide links via our sites directly to products like Dow Jones Interactive [35], Global Access [54], and Research Bank Web [135]. Those are the three fairly generic products that you'll use whether you're working at JP Morgan in New York or in Hong Kong or in Sydney or in London. Then we have additional services for different regions—for example, Reuters Business Briefing [115], a news database that we use extensively in Asia-Pacific and in Europe, isn't used at all in North America.

While we could have had a single intranet site for all the BRCs containing all the links that the various BRCs use, we decided to stick to having an individual BRC Web site for each location because there are differences in the resources that affect the choices that people make and what we would recommend.

The BRC in New York has put together a very useful guide which we call Research Tools. It provides information on all the major information databases available to investment banking staff globally. It's organised by category—news or local reports, brokers' estimates, that sort of thing—and within each category is a list of the products. We've given each product a grading based on whether we think it is a primary or secondary source, and little flags indicating which locations they're used in around the world. That has been very useful, since we have people transferring from country to country. For example, in New York they might use Nexis [98] for news, whereas if they come out here to Hong Kong, they would use Reuters Business Briefing. Research Tools globalises the options and points out the differences, all in a one-page guide.

It sounds like no single online resource could be considered the primary source around the world.

That's right. More and more, the online sources are becoming globally focused, but most of the databases are either U.S.- or European-centric. The Asia-Pacific region has been left in the cold, although the situation has improved dramatically in the past year or so, as the stock markets pick up and the online vendors realise there are huge opportunities out here for them. The big vendors also have the resources to extend their coverage.

Are there any free or low-cost Web sites that you often point people to when they're doing international research?

One site that we use a lot out here is IR Asia [77]. It has links to company Web pages, to documents, to information on industries, and one of the best things about the site is that it also has breaking announcements of financial results. When you're at the site, you can press the "refresh" button and get the latest interim results, for example, coming out from companies in the region.

You can even customise it so that you get free email alerts. You can link to stock quotes, professional associations, and regulatory bodies. That has been fantastic for us. We tell everybody about it, and it's featured very prominently on our BRC intranet site.

The other site that we like a lot is CorporateInformation.com [27]. We have found it to be quite good for coverage of Asian industries. It's free, it has the kind of investor relations information we're looking for, and people really do like using it. Unlike a lot of the global corporate Web sites, this one has very useful links to Asian information, especially on the industry side.

The stock exchange Web sites here are improving; more and more of them are providing coverage of corporate announcements and things like that. The Singapore Exchange [122] is especially good; it has been a leader in the region, providing not only the sort of information that you'd expect a stock exchange site to include, but also links to other valuable sites, regulatory authorities, and so on where available. The Hong Kong Exchange [63] has recently started pumping corporate announcements into its site, which is great, and long overdue. But we have problems with the Shenzhen and Shanghai stock exchanges, for instance, in China; their Web sites are only in Chinese, which we can't use at all. You can change your browser's character set so that the characters are displayed in Chinese, but you still have to be able to read Chinese.

What changes do you expect to see in the next few years in the field of international research?

I think that companies will increasingly recognise their role in the global business environment. In the past, they have been able to function quite effectively in their own marketplaces without being global in nature. But now they're beginning to realise that they have to change if they're going to compete at the global level and attract foreign investment.

We'll see improvements in the number of companies who provide English-language Web sites, and an increase in the amount of information they provide through those Web sites. One thing I have seen here recently is a large increase in the amount of foreign funds being invested in Asia, both on the asset management funds side and on the institutional and individual level, as people gain more access to information about markets around the world. They become more aware of opportunities in other regions. That has certainly been the case where they've recognised value in Asia, and they began investing here as the economies all started turning around. So, of course, it's in the interest of both the companies and the stock exchanges to provide rich Web sites and international information for investors.

The other trend I see is that, as the economies of smaller countries like Indonesia, Thailand, and Malaysia continue to improve, there will be more resources available for governments and corporations to invest in promoting their industries and businesses, and to support information sharing and Web site development projects.

Super Searcher Power Tips

➤ We have become more reliant on local Web sites rather than traditional databases, particularly for company information.

➤ You often have to think laterally: Okay, I can't get anything on this industry specifically, but what about companies in similar or related industries globally?

➤ Companies produce documents or information in their local language, and the big global databases may not include that content; it just gets dropped, and you'd never know you're missing it.

➤ You can train your clients, but at the end of the day, if you don't also make it easy for them to find things of value, then you're not really doing your job.

Michele Marinak

Global Information Consultant

Michele Marinak is a Consultant at Find/SVP in New York, NY. Find/SVP is a business advisory and research firm that provides business intelligence, marketing advice, and information consulting to 11,000 clients at more than 2,000 firms.

mmarinak@findsvp.com
www.findsvp.com

Why don't you start by telling me about your background and how you got started doing international research?

My academic background is as a historian, and I think that is a good match with the research profession. Throughout my academic career, I was involved with term papers, research projects, and academic investigation, or sleuthing, in general. After I graduated from Dartmouth, I worked for Research International, a large market research firm that is part of a group of companies called the WPP Group. While I was there, I did the traditional type of market research, large primary research surveys and studies and things like that, which brought in a business perspective. Then I moved to Find/SVP in March 1997 and started doing research consulting based on secondary research. So my background is a mix of two elements, first the research perspective and later the business mindset.

It must have been a big leap from history to market research.

You're right. It overlaps, though, in terms of the international sensibility, which has always been an interest of mine. The jump had been from studying international cultures and historical events to learning about international firms and current market issues. I think it's a good background in the sense that no matter how current or business-oriented the topic you're looking at, it's important to keep in mind the big picture of global cultural and historical differences. Methodologically, the two are also similar because they require you to investigate thoroughly, and to read and digest a great deal of information and then write about it concisely and clearly.

You see the similarities when you look at something like differences in information culture. For example, statistics that are tracked one way in the United States may not be tracked the same way in Latin America, and there's probably a reason for that. Companies may be organized in a certain way in the U.S., but completely differently in Europe. The executive mindsets are different and there are very different ways of negotiating in different cultures. In my academic career, I spent most of my time poring over thousands of pages of a historical text; now I seem to pore through thousands of Web pages or thousands of directory entries.

You mention being mindful of cultural differences. Do you run into that a lot in your international research, and if you do, do you recognize it before you get started, or do you stumble on it as you're going along?

I think it's a little of both. As you do more and more international research, some cultural differences become more obvious. But there are always surprises. In many cases you know from the outset, okay, this is not going to be tracked in the same way because the information culture in, say, Mexico is not the same as the information culture in the U.S. And it's possible that the market research industry, or the research or information-gathering industry in general, isn't at the same level of development.

Are there areas that are particularly fraught with those kinds of cultural disconnects? Are there types of questions that are more likely to not have answers in other information cultures?

Absolutely. In some sense, it's almost too obvious a pattern. When you look at the economic development of a nation as a whole, you often see a corresponding development of resources and information, and of the keeping and organizing of information. For example, the U.S. devotes resources to keeping statistics at a level that no other country does. If you go onto the Web sites of U.S. government agencies, you can spend a lifetime finding everything from the price of eggs in 1989 to the inflation rate in 1970. These kinds of things are tracked to an extraordinary level of detail on a very regular basis—in some cases and in some government agencies, on a monthly basis. It's not the same in a lot of other countries. The reasons are not always the same; sometimes it's as simple as the fact that countries don't have the resources to devote to such data-gathering—they're focused on basic development—or it may be that they choose not to make the information as readily available to the public as we do here.

A couple of types of questions cause red lights to go on in my head. I often encounter with clients a misconception of how unified the regions of the world are. People often call and ask, "Can you tell me about the market for automobiles in the U.S., Europe, and Latin America?" Well, okay, the U.S. is a single country and that makes it easy. Europe has made great strides in recent years toward unification, with the European Union and particularly now with the advent of the euro currency. But it's still not a single entity; there certainly are differences between Germany and Spain, for example. Further down the list in terms of unification is Latin America; there's not a whole lot of aggregate data available telling you how the auto industry is doing in Brazil *and* Paraguay *and* Chile *and* Guatemala.

I try to keep in mind at all times the different perspectives from which my clients are coming at their projects. At Find/SVP, I work with retainer client companies that vary from advertising and PR agencies, to consumer products companies, to consulting and financial firms. Their levels of savviness, both about the industry and companies that they may be asking about, and about research itself, vary.

In addition to different backgrounds in terms of the companies they work for, clients also vary in terms of their positions. Sometimes I'm working with other researchers and sometimes I'm working with marketing or sales people. I often run into situations in which people ask me about things that they admit they know nothing about. That's when a dialogue becomes important, a client-to-researcher conversation about what they are really trying to get at, what they know so far, and what I think will be available.

I worked on one project where that kind of dialogue was really important. This was a case where I didn't give the client what he'd asked for initially, but he walked away from the interaction feeling very satisfied with what I told him. In this case, the client asked how many closets there were in Latin America—you know, closets in people's homes. Frankly, I don't think anybody knows how many there are. I try to always assume that some information exists out there, but in this case I had serious doubts. What I ended up doing was having a discussion with the client about why he wanted to know and what he was hoping to get at. It turned out that he was interested in getting a general idea of the market for closet organizers in Latin America. Once I knew that, I could search for proximate indicators—statistics or information that I *could* find that would help him get an idea of the number of closets, and of what the market for closet organizers might be.

The information I ended up giving him was from companies like Euromonitor [42, see Appendix], the U.K. market research firm, with data like the average household size, the average number of rooms in a house. And from sources like the Inter-American Development Bank [72] and the World Bank [153], I got information on disposable income, which gave an indication of how many people would have the money to buy closet organizers, something that even in the U.S. I think is pretty clearly a discretionary purchase. Then I looked at other factors like shopping habits, which are tracked by retail consulting firms or consortia that study the retail industry. Nowadays, shopping habits are also tracked by people who are studying the Internet and e-commerce to find out how people who have this kind of money and this kind of space in their homes are shopping online.

That brings us to questions like whether affluent Latin Americans would be shopping in big cities in Latin America. Perhaps they would be shopping in big cities in the U.S. And that leads to questions about whether the client is really thinking of opening retail stores everywhere in Latin America, or whether he should think about starting in one country first and, if so, which one. The client ended up scratching his head at first, and then deciding that he had to focus his attention and pick one country to analyze in more depth.

That's something I've noticed over the past couple of years. People are appreciating the need for research more, the need for research at all levels. Secondary research is a really good start. When I did survey work for the primary research firm a few years back, I was shocked at how many people jumped into $40,000, $100,000, half-million dollar projects studying a new advertisement or a response to a new product, without doing preliminary background research into market conditions. I think that's changing now; as people realize how much information is out there, they come to understand how important it is to have that information work for them.

I'm struck by how much added value information professionals provide when they conduct a thorough reference interview. In that example, your job was to help your client focus on what he was trying to accomplish, what his goal was, and what information he really needed.

Right; our job is to probe in those kinds of ways, and people have different reactions to that. In some cases, they are a little bit shocked and they think, "Why would you want to know this?" They may be concerned about confidentiality, or too pressed for time to discuss what they need on the phone. But, once you're able to engage somebody in true back-and-forth dialogue, they realize that you'll be able to find more information if they tell you more background.

That's part of the evolution of the research profession, from looking for facts or finding articles, to dispensing expertise, distilling information, and, for lack of a better word, providing solutions. I think it's hard for members of our profession to mentally take that step up, to see ourselves as an added-value proposition as opposed to people who just do research in its simpler sense.

The firm where I work is a good microcosm, because we have clients who still call and want what they would call a data dump. They'll say, "Send me all the articles that appeared about this company or this industry in the past six months, and I'll just weed through them." On the other end, we have people who really want analysis and bullet points and more of a distillation or "best of the best" report.

Can you describe a typical international research question?

To oversimplify a bit, my projects fall into four basic categories. One kind of research I do—and this isn't unique to being an international researcher—deals with questions about companies. Clients call and ask me to tell them about the financial performance of this Swiss company, or the new product development of that German company, or the advertising and marketing plans of this Japanese company, or the recent acquisitions of a particular Brazilian company. It's company research around the world, with varied motivations—clients looking for potential acquisition targets, or learning about their international competitors as they start to think about expanding abroad.

Another type of research I do is industry research. I have people asking about the publishing industry in Japan, or the automotive aftermarket in Mexico, or the world market for, well, you can fill in the blanks. Sometimes it is as obscure as rotary pumps, and sometimes it is as straightforward as automobiles.

A third type of research involves more general country information. For example, I'll get a call from a client who is thinking about opening a factory somewhere in Europe; maybe they're thinking about Germany and maybe they're thinking about the Netherlands. They want to know about government attitudes toward foreign investment and whether or not the governments have regulations or incentives that encourage it. They need to find out about the transportation infrastructure. They want to learn about the local work force and the cost of living.

Other times it's even more basic. A client is thinking about starting to sell products in Thailand but doesn't know much about the country. He or she wants to know where the economy is right now and where it's predicted to go in the next couple of years. Clients ask about anything from the level of involvement of the government in business to the economic state of affairs.

The fourth type of research we do is true economic statistical research for clients who are asking about inflation, or GDP (gross domestic product), or consumer prices, or wages around the world.

What do you do when the sources themselves are in a language other than English?

Well, you try to learn as many languages as you can. I speak fluent Spanish, and I read Portuguese and Italian. I can speak enough of those languages to order food and wine—the essentials!—or to ask on the phone if I can be directed to someone who speaks English. I'm about to embark on learning French, too.

If the sources aren't in one of those languages, I've begun to rely more on some of the Web translation services that offer free translations of web sites on the single-word level or in some cases even page-length. I've used Babelfish [201] and Dictionary.com [34], and there are some others that I use for particular languages. I would put a big asterisk next to this, though, and say that I don't place my complete faith in them yet, and I may never.

Luckily, I have colleagues who speak some other languages, so I rely on them whenever possible. In some cases, I have also turned to government sources, or to people in consulates, embassies, or trade promotion societies in the New York area—people who work for government agencies in our local area for the purpose of promoting business between the U.S. and their country. Sometimes they're willing to be helpful if they can see the benefits that helping me might bring to their government and their country's economy.

What changes have you seen over the last few years in the resources available for international research?

I've seen a couple of things. One is that there are more sources than there used to be. I do some projects for clients now in very short order that, a couple of years ago, would have had me scratching my head and throwing up my hands. I wouldn't have been able to do very much. As the pace of globalization quickens and competition drives firms to look for new places to buy, make, and sell goods and services, there is more of a market for the collection of details about other countries. More companies need information about other nations and so more companies are putting it together and selling it.

Another big trend is the movement of information to the Internet, for better or for worse. And I am not only talking about new Internet sources, but also about sources that have been around for a while moving to a Web interface. Dow Jones Interactive [35] has moved from a software product to a Web-based product. Dialog [33] now has a Web interface. You used to have to use proprietary software to access LexisNexis [88], but now it's available through the Internet. That's a big change. It makes life a little easier, since I don't have to run all the specialized software packages on my PC. On the other hand, when our Internet connection is slow or the server is down, I think our entire company lets out a collective yelp.

It's important to make sure that your palette of research tools stays diversified. As archaic as it sounds, I still keep paper files of seminal articles at my desk. You know the kind I mean; if I did search literature on this topic, I would never find this great chart, or this fabulous list, or what have you, because the title of the article isn't very indicative of the subject, or the first paragraph doesn't say anything useful, or I can't be sure that the graphics would be preserved in the proper format.

What do you think is the hardest thing about doing global research?

A couple of things make it trickier than doing domestic research. One is that the universe is just that much larger, so truly global research is still pretty difficult. As of now, and for the foreseeable future, most industries are not completely global, even with all the changes in that direction brought about by factors like the Internet. That makes it tricky, because trying to create a global picture is just that—it's trying to create something that doesn't exist; you often just don't find information that is as comprehensive as you would like it to be. The other problem, which we touched on earlier, is the difference among information cultures and in what is available in various countries.

Sometimes you just have to find the closest indicator of whatever it is you're looking for. You learn all about proximate indicators like the ones I used in that closet organizer project, all about looking for something close: If we can't find the data for the world, let's see if we can identify which countries are the biggest players in the industry, or let's see if we can find out who the five biggest companies in the industry are, and look at them.

In a similar vein, how do you know when you're done? When you're looking for information in a country or region that you're not familiar with, and you don't have a list of "usual suspects," how do you know when you've done a thorough job?

It depends. Sometimes you know because, as with more familiar research, you start to run into the same information again and again, or you realize that you're just not finding anything more. Sometimes you know because someone helps you out. That may be someone from a trade organization or some other kind of expert, someone who has more knowledge of that industry or that company than you do. Sometimes it just comes down to instinct and making a judgment call, thinking about the difference between academic research and business research, and keeping in mind that our relationship with our clients is one in which we're looking for best-efforts information. So sometimes I come to a point where I think, "Okay, I've sunk three hours into this and I've got 80 percent of what I was looking for. If I sink another ten hours into this project, maybe I will have 100 percent. Maybe."

That's the case with global research; sometimes you can never be completely sure that you've really gotten to that point. But that's where the dialogue with the client comes back into play. It is very important to talk at the beginning of the project, but it's also important to talk at the point where you're ready to deliver something to your client. You have to say, "Okay, this is what I've done so far. If I had to do more, maybe I could do this. What do you think? Is this enough of a picture for you? How comprehensive does this need to be? Maybe what you'd like to do instead is pick out some elements from what I've already done and look at them in closer detail, look at a little smaller piece of the puzzle, but in greater depth."

Have you noticed any patterns in the amount of global information you find on the open Web as opposed to the amount you find in the fee-based services?

It varies. If I had to draw an average across all the kinds of research we do, I would say that less than 30 percent of what I do comes from the free Internet, 50 percent comes from fee-based electronic resources, and 20 percent comes from other places, which could be telephone calls to trade organizations or government sources, or print publications such as directories and other resources that haven't made it online yet.

Do you have any favorite print resources that you use to get started on a research project?

It's tricky, because the companies or industries a client asks me to research may be ones that I don't know very much about. My area of expertise is in understanding international markets and knowing about international sources, but I might not know anything about a particular industry. If I get a call from someone who wants information on industrial equipment or the aquaculture market, the print sources that I turn to are ones that tell me about those industries in big, broad, sweeping brushstrokes. One resource that I often use is *The Encyclopedia of Global Industries* [173]. There are a few directories of international publications, such as *Benn's Media* [162] and *International Media*

Guides [188], that I use to look up newsletters or to find the key magazines in an industry or a country.

I use a couple of print sources from Euromonitor almost daily, for basic statistical information on things like market sizes and retail sales of particular goods—anything from population to income to the size of households in Latin America, which I needed for that closets project. The ones I use all the time are Euromonitor's *International Marketing Data and Statistics* [187] and *European Marketing Data and Statistics* [175], as well as *Consumer Europe* [167] and *Consumer International* [168]. I often use a publication from Dun & Bradstreet called the *D&B Exporters' Encyclopaedia* [170], which is replete with information for companies that are thinking of exporting, although I use it primarily for contact names. For each country, it has a fabulous list of both domestic and local information sources, from consulates to business information sources to trade promotion organizations.

Do you use any Web-based portals or aggregator sites for your research?

Yes. For example, if I'm doing research on Latin America, I might start with government sources like the Inter-American Development Bank and the UN Economic Commission for Latin America and the Caribbean [139]. I will also look at sources like LatinFocus [87] and the Latin American Newsletters [85] sites. University sites like those provided by the University of Texas' Latin American Network Information Center [84] can also be useful. These provide not only their own information, but also links to other places for either regional or country-level data.

The same is true for Europe. I might start with the European Union's Web site [45]. It certainly is a very comprehensive site, and it is sometimes a good place to start for regional European Union industry data. But the site itself is very difficult to use. The EU also has a print publication called the *Panorama of EU Industry* (now renamed *Monthly Panorama of European*

Business [191]), and the falloff in terms of content and user-friendliness between the 1997 edition and the 1999 edition is appalling. But this comes back to the point I was making earlier about keeping your mind open to non-online sources; the EU has an office in New York, and they're really helpful. If you call them, they curse the EU Web site too, and they help you find what you need.

What about fee-based online sources? Are there any that you find particularly useful?

There are a couple I really like. One is fairly low-cost and is produced by the U.S. Department of Commerce, called the National Trade Data Bank [96]. That's a useful place to start for market research reports prepared by in-country Foreign Commercial Service officers. If you can find a report that is current, it's often a bullseye for your client. For example, if you're looking at toys in Germany and a Commercial Officer has written a report within the last year, that's usually a great big bonus, because the report will have market information as well as names of players and contacts. It's a wonderful find.

Other, more expensive, fee-based sources that I use a lot are still the old standbys. Dialog has a big place in my basket of tricks as a place to find directory entries and company financials as well as market research reports and press articles. I use Reuters Business Briefing [115] every day as a source for press coverage in English as well as local languages. Dow Jones Interactive is occasionally useful, too, although it is more domestically focused. DJI is actually in the throes of a merger with Reuters Business Briefing to form a new product called Factiva. I have tested this one out, but think it still needs some work. So, I'll use the NTDB for its market research database, Reuters primarily for press articles, and Dialog for press, market research, and some company information.

I use some other online sources for more specific company-oriented information. I'll search Hoover's [64], FIS Online [50], which is where you'll find *Moody's Reports,* and Bureau van Dijk's Amadeus [6] database for similarly detailed financials about private European companies. I also go to sources of analysts' reports, like Investext (now Thomson Financial Securities Data [135]) and Multex [95].

How do you stay up to date on new sources, particularly those outside the U.S.?

I rely on industry conferences, both those that focus on research and those that are more oriented toward international markets. Because I work in a large firm, there's a collective brain trust that I can tap into. We have people who go to SCIP [214] conferences, American Marketing Association [207] workshops, and conferences like Internet Librarian [211] and Online World, now replaced by Web Search University [216] and eContent Expo [210]. Find/SVP people go to conferences in the technology industry and the marketing industry, and when they come back, we pool our collective knowledge base. Of course, we also have librarians on staff here who keep track of events and new resources, and they point out items that come across their desks that might be of interest to us. For example, the library referred me to someone from SkyMinder [123], which was a new international information source for me. I will investigate it in the coming weeks and decide if it is something we should add to our collection.

Are there any publications or email lists that you find useful for keeping on top of new sources?

As a matter of fact, Find/SVP publishes a periodical that I find useful, *The Information Advisor* [181]. Other than that, no, I don't know of any email lists that focus on announcing new international research sources. I wish I did! Most of the email lists I subscribe to don't have a solely international focus, but come instead from reputable news sources like *The New York Times* and the *Economist,* or research companies like eMarketer [40] and MindBranch [93].

What trends do you see in international research? What do you think you'll be doing differently in three or four years?

I think we'll see more of the move I mentioned, from being people who find information to being people who provide expertise. First, we'll have to develop our technical skills as researchers, and second, we'll have to develop more familiarity with international markets. This evolution will continue because the amount of information that is becoming available will continue to increase toward infinity. As people become more time-crunched, they'll need more help. They'll need someone to distill, filter, package, format, and sometimes spoon-feed the information to them. What we need to do is make information actionable. We will have an increasing number of tools to work with, and it will be more and more about honing the craft, knowing the best sources and how to use them to get what you need, and knowing how to turn the raw materials into a final product.

I've always thought that one of the least-appreciated talents of information professionals is our almost unconscious ability to figure out what is a reliable information source.

Yes, our skill is in knowing which sources are good and figuring out how to teach that to our clients. In many ways, the Internet is a researcher's best friend. If clients are left to their own devices to play around on the Internet for long enough, they'll realize just what a time sink the Internet is. That's when they come to us as researchers. We can teach them that there are two parts to finding information on the Net: locating the information, and knowing whether you can trust it.

Any other thoughts on how to be an expert international researcher?

Make sure you keep current. Try not to get into too much of a pattern or a rut about the sources that you use. It's important to be familiar with the sources that you can always count on and that will always provide certain types of information, but it's good to keep your mind open to other ways of doing things, too. That applies to all kinds of research, as a matter of fact.

Also, I've read this a hundred times, from a hundred different sources, but it's important to always ask yourself at the beginning of every project, "Who would know? Who has already studied this and what is the quickest, most comprehensive way to find out what they know?" If the information already exists in some collected form, it doesn't make sense to reinvent the wheel. That's the best way to get an initial grasp on where to go. Before you dive headfirst into a research project, stick a toe in, test the water a bit and think, "How do I want to approach this? What's the best way?"

Always keep in mind the issue of reliability of sources. And if you're working for a client, it's important to keep in mind the time versus money continuum. The most important thing I learn every day is how key the dialogue with the client is. It is crucial to understand why you're looking for what you're looking for, what level of detail they need, and what familiarity they already have with the research topic. That way you can figure out whether what they say initially is really what they are looking for, or if you can provide them with something else that will be of even more help to them.

Super Searcher Power Tips

➤ I try to always assume that some information exists, even if I have to just look for proximate indicators—statistics or information I can find that would help the client get an idea.

➤ The Internet is a researcher's best friend. If clients are left to their own devices, they realize just what a time sink the Internet is. That's when they come to us as researchers.

➤ Try not to get into too much of a rut about the sources you use. Keep your mind open to other ways of doing things.

➤ It's important to make sure that your palette of research tools stays diversified. As archaic as it sounds, I still keep paper files of seminal articles at my desk.

➤ The most important thing that I learn every day is how important the dialogue with the client is.

➤ The research profession is evolving, from looking for facts or finding articles to dispensing expertise, distilling information, and providing solutions.

Desmond Crone

London-Based Financial Information Executive

Desmond Crone is an information executive at Schroder Salomon Smith Barney in London, supporting the Financial Institutions Group in the investment bank.

djjb.crone@virgin.net

To start with, can you tell me about your background?

I did a history degree, and I didn't know what to do after college. I worked for a year in a public library and discovered the world of information, and then went on to do a post-graduate diploma in library and information studies at the University of Wales, Aberystwyth. During that course I heard about business information and corporate libraries, so as soon as the course had finished, I came to London and applied for various jobs and did some temping work around the city. I ended up working at Coopers and Lybrand, and since then I've worked at a number of banks and consulting and advisory firms. In July 1999, I joined the financial institutions advisory team at Schroder's Corporate Finance, and in May 2000, Schroder's Investment Bank became part of the Salomon Smith Barney investment banking business of CitiGroup.

I joined Schroder's Financial Institution Group, or FIG, to manage the research and information for their team of bankers.

It was a group of about thirty-five bankers of various nationalities, based in London but with teams in Paris, Frankfurt, and New York as well. There is quite a range of nationalities among the bankers—Irish, Portuguese, Spanish, Italian, German, Austrian, French, Russian, even an American. Since I started, it has grown to about sixty bankers, and they are planning to grow it to something like eighty within a year.

But when I started, the team had got to a size that they felt merited their own information person running research projects for them and also looking at managing their internal information a bit. So I am sort of an internal consultant as well as a research person. I advise them on how to manage, store, and track presentations and client files and that kind of thing. I am pretty much the only person providing research for my FIG team. There is a corporate library as well, and I work with them, and when I can't handle everything because of workloads, I involve them.

Can you describe a typical international research project?

A typical project would be something like sizing the banking markets for a range of countries. Often that would be European countries, in which case that's not so impossible to do, because most of the European nations are G-10 economy, for example. They're covered by the Bank for International Settlements [13, see Appendix] and the OECD (Organisation for Economic Co-operation and Development) [103], so there are sources to answer that kind of question.

The project might be to size the banking markets over a range of economies and then to make some sort of measure of concentration of the market and get a ranking of the top players, and then work out what percentage of assets or deposits in that banking system might be accounted for by the top five or the top ten institutions.

That's all fairly possible when you're talking about Europe. It's more of a pain when it's Asia Pacific or Latin America, because the Bank for International Settlements or the European Central Bank [44] data doesn't extend that far. So you end up digging around in the Central Bank's Web pages and calling up banks, and digging around in IMF [75] data series.

The next step is to try to get growth projections for how the markets are going to move, and to try to build up time series and a picture over time. That I always find incredibly difficult, because no two organisations do the same sorts of projections or measure the same things. You wonder how valuable those numbers are when they are so inconsistent, but bankers seem to like them.

It sounds like you're doing a fair amount of analysis as well as gathering of the data.

Yes, that's why I chose the Schroder's opportunity. It promised to be the kind of job where I would have room to do more than just gather data and hand it over to someone else; I actually have a role in distilling some value out of the data that I've found. I wish I had more time for that distillation, but I'm only one person and I have sixty bankers to look after. I am helping them on the more basic-level questions as well, like finding out if it's possible to get financials for a Serbian bank or whatever. Maybe 5 to 10 percent of my time is spent doing analysis, and I would be happier if it was closer to 50 percent of my time.

Do your research techniques change when you look for information outside Europe?

I've got my information map for Europe, and I know roughly what's possible and how to go about getting ahold of that type of information. When I'm looking at someplace like Latin America or an Asian country, then I'm much more in the dark. I just have to do the obvious information things like look in the *Europa World Year Book* [174] and get the telephone number for the Central Bank, then look for the Central Bank Web page, and try to find an association to email or fax. The further away from Europe I go, the greyer it is for me.

How do you evaluate information sources when you get into those greyer areas and you can't rely on the standard resources that you know and love?

The only thing that I can do is try to find a second or third source to corroborate the information, and then usually you just end up with three different sets of numbers. That often happens even in the markets that you know well. You find three sources and you've got three completely different sets of numbers; that's a problem for the banker in trying to work out which set of numbers is reliable.

And how do you handle looking for information when the sources are in a language that you don't speak?

I have been trying very hard for the last ten years to learn Italian, so I've got a clue with Italian and some of the other Romance languages. And because I've been focused on the FIG areas for four years now, I know quite a lot of the key words in the different languages; I know what a word like "insurance" would look like in various languages. So, for example, if I were in a German site, I'd look for the word Versicherung, or in a Dutch site, I would look for the word Verzekerings or Verzekeraars. I know I'm on the right track if I find a table and it says Versicherung and it's got a list of company names; I know that's got to be the ranking or something to do with insurance.

But you're right, language is a huge problem. Once the research starts moving into Middle Eastern and Asia Pacific countries where they have completely different alphabets, then you have to rely on the source publishing in English as well as in the native language; obviously, that's going to cut down how much of a window you have into the information.

When you run into something like that, do most of your users understand the limitations? Do they expect you to find the material for Middle East countries just as fantastically as you managed to find them for Italy, for example?

When I worked for a consulting firm, this was quite a problem. The consultants used to live with this image of the perfect world, where they came up with the perfect question and they'd want me to come up with the perfect answer. The bankers seem to live more in the real world; if you can explain your research, and you can show them the steps that you've taken, and if they can't add anything to that, they're usually really happy with what you've done. I do find that to be a difference between bankers and consultants, at least in my experience. The bankers certainly seem to listen to what you have to say about why there's a problem, and what you did about it, and what the result was.

Do you use any of the online translation services?

I only use AltaVista's Babelfish [201]. I really have found that useful with languages like German that I have absolutely no clue about. But I suppose that's part of the value in being part of a group of so many nationalities—there's usually somebody around whom you can show something to and ask, "Is this the sort of thing I'm looking for? What does this say? Should I pass this on to my client?"

What changes have you seen in information sources over the last few years?

As others have said, the Web has changed everything. A lot of the books and CD-ROM sources that we used a few years ago are now only on the Web. For example, the credit research from the ratings agencies such as Standard & Poor's [125] and Moody's [94] has all crossed over to Web-only versions. They're leaving the hard copy behind, and I guess they'll be leaving the CD-ROM channel behind as well.

The concern that we have is that, as information sources are moving onto the Web and tweaked so that they are easy to use for an end-user who doesn't use that product day in and day out, they are getting dumbed down and becoming less flexible and less functional. The danger is that we'll end up with all these glossy, end-user-oriented systems that don't deliver the same functionality that people who grew up in the online era expect.

A good example of that is Research Bank Web [135]; instead of using the Thomson interface to the Investext [135] database, I end up running my searches on the Dow Jones Interactive [35] or the Dialog [33] version of the database, just so that I have that functionality and search power.

Back when all we had was dial-up access to Investext, I was able to do very precise searches that would save me quite a lot of time in tracking down the pages that I wanted to read. Now it doesn't seem to work quite so well. You would think that the vendor's interface would be designed to take advantage of all the features of the product—that Research Bank Web would be a better product to search than the corresponding files on Dow Jones or Dialog—but it doesn't turn out to be the case. You end up using Dow Jones or Dialog because you know you can be more flexible and fit more brackets in the search strategy, and that sort of thing. It just seems to work better, somehow. .xls [159] have done the same thing—they have found that they can add value by adding in more indexing than Thomson has.

Another thing—and it's odd because it is the opposite of what one would have expected with all the consolidation of vendors and aggregators that has taken place—is the fact that you still have lots and lots of places to look through. Take analysts' research notes, for example. There are CD-ROM databases to look at, there's the Web version to look at, there's Multex [95] to look at. There are in-house databases to look at as well. And then you discover that each of those places actually has different coverage of the data. I found a broker the other day whose reports were only on the CD version of Research Bank and not on the Web, which completely destroyed my assumption that when I've done my search on the Web version, I have done enough. You need to check the CD version as well, just in case that particular broker is not on the Web but is on the CD version of the database. You end up doing five searches instead of one. Three or four years ago, when all those information companies were buying each other, while I thought that prices would go up, I thought that at least the efficiency and the time required to find the information would improve. But that hasn't happened yet.

I do think that the aggregators and vendors—Reuters, Thomson, Reed Elsevier—have done a very good job of bringing together the English-language sources and content, but what is frustrating is that the non-English-language material is usually quite separate and not aggregated into the rest of the material. It's still very country specific. For example, Reuters Business Briefing [115] and LexisNexis [88] have new sources in German, French, Italian, Spanish, and so on, and that's fine, but their coverage only extends to news sources. When you're looking for industry data or market research or analysts' reports, you always come up against the fact that the only information you will get online is going to be in English. To actually get local industry market data, you need to subscribe to the local print magazines, and you need a native-speaking banker or somebody to go through each issue and spot tables and other useful lists of largest fund managers or largest insurance companies or whatever.

What do you do when you do get a request for which you feel you need to dig beyond what you can find in the commercial online databases?

With luck, you have a subscription to the print magazine that covers the topic. For example, for German insurance there is the

VersicherungsWirtschaft magazine with good industry analysis of German industry; for Spanish insurance there is *Actualidad Aseguradora*, and for French insurance there is *L'Argus*. So you can start by looking through the print publications and hoping to get at the originators of the data by talking to the associations in those countries.

I have the advantage of working with bankers who come from those countries, so they sometimes have an inkling of a source for the information. Sometimes they will remember that a certain newspaper always covers the topic, or that a particular association tracks statistics in this area. If you haven't got that kind of community of knowledge, and if you haven't got the hard copy of the appropriate magazine, and if you ring the association on the day it's closed, or you talk to the wrong person or whatever, then you've missed it—that's all.

You must run into time limitations, too, with bankers needing things yesterday?

Well, this is an interesting thing about not being in the corporate library but actually sitting with the team. Back in the days when I worked in the library, I would have a deadline of an hour or two to turn the request around and deliver it. Now, since I'm actually sitting with the bankers in the business unit, I notice that the same questions keep coming back and coming back and coming back. So, yes, I do have that time constraint of the really stupid deadline or the impossible mission, but I also can think, "Well, I'll order this anyway, even though it won't arrive for another ten days." When it does come in, I can take it along to the banker and check to see if it's still useful, and often it isn't too late after all. And even if they can't use it for the particular client's job that they were working on, it's still going to be useful information. I find that a very rewarding aspect of sitting where I do. It's a matter of having enough of a focus on my client base and spending all my time with the bankers. Even if you miss their initial deadline, sometimes you discover that it wasn't the real deadline anyway.

Do you find that you can anticipate their questions, just because you're closer to them and working with them all day?

That's the idea behind my going to their weekly meetings, to have a feel for what business is coming up and what's on their minds. But in fact I haven't found myself being particularly proactive in that way. I do a current awareness bulletin each day, and I think they find that helpful. And simply the fact that very often we've had the same or a very similar question on an area or a country before means that I've got some clues about how it went last time. You kind of build a database of experience, so you can avoid some of the dead-end roads that you went down before. You know that's not where the answer is, so you can cut down the time it takes to find the information.

Do you encounter many situations where the banker's question comes with certain cultural assumptions about what information can be found?

Oh, yes. While I was at Morgan Stanley, I remember the Americans used to come over from New York and say, "We have all this, this, and this for North America, so we need to get the same information for Europe." They had a real problem adjusting to the fact that things are different here. They did adjust fairly quickly to the European reality of having to look up ten sources in different languages, with different levels of detail and coverage in each country. But they would come in and ask, "Why can't I find this person's home address?" And you have to explain that, well, this is the Nordic market, and they have very strict laws regarding privacy and data protection. More recently, my experience has been Europeans saying, "I've got this wonderful table showing me in-flows for asset managers in the States; I want this for Europe." And it can't be done, or at least not to the same extent.

But the idea of cultural blind spots works a little bit in reverse here, too—we have cultural blind spots about research outside the U.K. and Europe. In the U.K., even if companies are privately held, they have to make public their financial statements, whereas in the States if a company is private, that's it. You can get a credit rating and a credit report, which might have some clues, but information on how the business is doing financially—that's between the owners and the Internal Revenue Service. It's a bit of a surprise to realise that we can get only minimal information on large U.S. companies like Cargill.

How do you know when you've done a complete search? How do you know when to stop?

In my situation, I don't ever really stop. I file away the projects that didn't come to a satisfactory conclusion. I tell myself to just keep an eye out for anything else that might be useful. Oddly enough, there does seem to be kind of a serendipity about these things. If you have looked for something, and bashed your head against all the brick walls you could find, and done everything you could, and talked to everyone you could think of, then two weeks later you'll see a little snippet in *The Wall Street Journal Europe* or in the *Financial Times* or in an industry magazine. Sometimes, that's how life is.

You've done everything you possibly can on a search, and you've written it up and explained to everyone all the things that you've done, and no one can second-guess you or point out a source you missed. At that point, you close it off. But I always remember those sorts of things and I look out for little opportunities, and sometimes that little opportunity pops up.

How do you stay updated on new sources for information?

I'm really not very good at this at all, I have to confess. At the consulting firm where I used to work, we would get all the magazines from America, like *Online* [192] and *EContent* [172], plus the U.K. ones, like *What's New in Business Information* [200]. There would be a big stack of them going around from everyone's in-tray to everyone else's in-tray. At Schroder's and at Salomon, we don't have that, and I think we probably should. Mostly, I rely on Free Pint [178]. It has the discussion forum where you can stick your requests up in front of everyone, and there's the email newsletter. And I attend the Online Information exposition [212] in December in London, but I don't even go to that every year. The most useful way I've found to stay updated is just to keep talking to all the people I've worked with in the past, maintaining my network of contacts. I have the sense that maybe there aren't that many new things coming up in terms of content.

Do you use any of the country-specific search engines when you're doing international research?

Hardly ever, I must confess. What I tend to do is go to MetaCrawler [92] and just stick my words in and see what comes up; occasionally I stumble across something really good from, say, Spain or Italy, and I just follow that through. Very rarely do I use a country-specific search engine, though.

What free Web information resources do you find critical?

I love the International Federation of Stock Exchanges [74]. It has all the market sizing data for the stock exchanges around the world; it's fantastic. If I've got a question about stock exchanges, about size, trends, index levels, trading, velocity, that sort of thing, I find this site to be wonderful. But you have to have the right questions for it; it's not perfect. For market studies, I use MarketResearch.com [90], which is an index of market research reports. Sometimes that lets you identify a research house or a market study in an economy in which you have no idea who the main players are.

What about the professional online services? Which sources do you find critical to your day-to-day work?

I love TableBase [130]. You don't always find what you like to find, but very often you'll find one little table which will give you the names of the four or five companies that you're looking for. It can often answer that nagging question in two minutes and for just $8, and you think, "Wow, that saved so much time, and here's the answer." Then there are the standard online sources like OneSource [102], Reuters Business Briefing, Dow Jones Interactive, LexisNexis, and Investext, which we use pretty much all the time. For financials, if you can't find it in the Amadeus [6] file on Bureau van Dijk, then DataStar [31] has a good selection of financial databases for various countries.

Another source we use all the time is BankScope [14], also available from Bureau van Dijk. There is a bit of a gap waiting to be filled for similar products for insurers. AM Best [5], Bureau van Dijk, and Thomson are competing to fill that gap, but I don't think a solid product exists yet that gives comprehensive coverage of the insurance industry around the world.

And what print sources do you rely on?

I'm always going back to the *Europa World Year Book*. That's the main print resource I rely on.

Where do you think international research is going in the next few years?

I think it's going to be more of the same; more and more information on everyone's desktop and on the Web, and maybe we'll be able to wave goodbye to our modems and do everything on the Web through high-speed networks. Hopefully in the fairly near future, newspapers like the *Financial Times* that don't seem to care about preserving the tables and the graphics that they happily publish in their hard copy editions, will make more of an effort to store them and make them accessible on the Web. Dow Jones Interactive is better at doing that, but I think the *Financial Times* needs to work just a bit harder. So often the gold is in the graphics and tables, but the newspaper publishers often leave them out when they transfer the text to online.

And I expect to see more publisher/vendor/aggregator con-solidation. They've still got to tackle the language issue and address the need for geographically specific resources.

Do you have any other advice for doing international research?

Yes. Never think that you know the answer, even if you've done this question five or six times before. I tend to tell myself, "I know my way around this problem and I know what the answer's going to be." But I always think it's best to look at it afresh, to look for the new angle; maybe you'll have an extra special breakthrough this time. And often enough you do. That is why I still love being a researcher; you never really know the answer fully. There's always another angle, there's always a bit more information you can find out about a topic. And that could even be information that completely negates all the things that you knew before.

The other advice I would give is to make the most of all the people you've worked with in the past, and maintain your net-work. Email is such a boon for that, being able to just fire off a few top-of-the-mind questions: "What does anyone think about this?" or "Has this come up for anyone else in your group?" Often this is so handy, because other people have had the same ques-tions and very often they've got an answer, and you can all share and learn from that. You make yourself part of a virtual team.

Super Searcher Power Tips

➤ For Latin America or an Asian country, I look in the *Europa World Year Book* and get the telephone number for the Central Bank, then look for the Central Bank Web page, and try to find an association to email or fax.

➤ The big challenges are language issues—getting access to the local sources that would have all this wonderful data that you need but aren't available online—and the privacy restrictions on what information is available in different countries and regions.

➤ I have found AltaVista's Babelfish really useful with languages like German that I have absolutely no clue about.

➤ The most useful way I've found to stay updated on new sources is just to keep talking to all the people I've worked with in the past, maintaining my network of contacts.

➤ Never think that you know the answer, even if you've done this question five or six times before. It's best to look at it afresh, to look for the new angle; maybe you'll have an extra special breakthrough this time.

Arnoldo Sterinzon

Argentine Information Specialist

Arnoldo Sterinzon is principal and owner of Ontymel B Latin American Business Information, in Buenos Aires, Argentina. Ontyme IB provides customized strategic research, document delivery, and clipping services for clients.

arnoldo@ontymeib.com
www.ontymeib.com

First, can you tell me about your background and how you decided to start your business?

I studied in Buenos Aires and received my high level degree in business administration at the Facultad de Ciencias Economicas in the Universidad de Buenos Aires. I still live in Buenos Aires. As for how I got into the independent research business, years ago I was working as a manager at a telephone PABX manufacturer. In the evenings, I did research with a very old Commodore 64 computer, and I used the results of my research at work. Then in 1989 I said to myself, "If I can do this kind of online research for other people's businesses, why can't I do it for my own business?"

I spent a year planning and setting up the business. That included creating and incorporating the company, designing a logo, building a brochure, collecting all the contact lists, etc. I also took a trip to the States; I attended the Online '89 conference and went to several seminars, including Sue Rugge's [213, see Appendix] information brokering seminar. I subscribed to various online magazines, I read books, and so on. I sold my old motorbike and put all my investments in this risky venture that nobody here in Argentina knew anything about.

When I think back, I remember that when I was quite young, twelve or fourteen years old, I would listen to shortwave radio stations with very old equipment, during late-night hours after school, sports, girlfriends, and so on. I listened to radio broadcasts from around the world. I even heard the next day's news before everybody in the country did. I see a lot in common between listening to shortwave radio stations and running a research business, because they both involve seeking out information wherever it may be, and working across time zones and, sometimes, late into the night.

For professional development, I try to fly to the States as often as I can, to attend conferences, exhibitions, and meetings. It is a ten-hour flight, but it is worth the trip. I'm the only independent researcher in this region. I'm sure I'm not the only independent researcher in Argentina, but there are only a few of us. I find it so useful to establish contacts with colleagues and to attend the AIIP [208] annual conference when I can. And while I wouldn't say I started at the same time as AIIP, I began my business close to the same time that the organization was founded in 1987.

How much of your work now involves international research?

International research is about 70 percent of our total activity. We are focused mainly on Latin American business information research, and we cover the full continent, from Mexico down to here in Argentina, with contacts in every country. Between 60 and 80 percent of our clients are from outside the country; mainly they are located in the States and Europe. I do work for a number of fellow AIIP members. In terms of the kind of work we do, it is about half online research and half manual research, talking to experts and working with our network of contacts.

Can you describe a typical international research project?

We've changed our focus during the ten years since the business began. Right now, a typical project might be for a company interested in a partnership with an established business in this region. So they would need information in order to analyze locations and figure out where to focus their investments. We cover due diligence issues, lawsuits, competitive intelligence, companies' business structures, etc.

Another example might be researching a specific market covering several countries. We would get company reports, market data, and financial information. There are a lot of examples on our Web site of the types of research we do—investigating business opportunities, identification of market niches, document delivery, ongoing clipping services to keep customers updated on new market potential, and so on.

People talk a lot about global research, and I think that the Latin American region is particularly a subject of research these days. Latin America is a target for many companies worldwide, in terms of new investment opportunities. So our research often includes a group of countries—Argentina, Brazil, and Chile or Mexico, Brazil, and Peru.

In addition to investment information, we often need to provide information to help the client understand the market. So we become almost a partner of the company, first understanding very clearly what they need the information for, and then helping them understand the context of the information we provide. Our clients consider it very important that we are in the region. We are not sitting at a desk in New York, let's say, and doing research on Brazil. We have a person in Brazil who speaks Portuguese, and who understands the market, the local culture, and who the main players and the leading companies are.

What changes have you seen in international research over the last few years?

The biggest change, in this region in particular, is the fact that so much more information is available through the Internet now. This has helped us go directly to the information and reduce the turnaround time. In many cases, in the past, we needed a local contact in the area. Now, we can often get the information online.

Unfortunately, though, most of the information is in English; you don't find many Spanish-language databases. Even the material created by Latin American sources is in English, because most online vendors are American companies. So they take the magazine articles and translate them into English. But we add value for our clients by analyzing the database content we retrieve, and by providing manual research to supplement our database searching.

Have you seen the same trend toward electronic information with government sources?

Forget about government information! If you need government information, most of the time it has to be retrieved manually, by someone located in the area. I would say that Brazil, Chile, Argentina, Mexico, and, in a sense, Peru are the countries that are doing a good job at collecting information and making it available online. But the rest of the countries are not very clear in their policies about what's to be put on the Internet.

Fortunately, the major magazines and newspapers put at least the indexes to most of their information online. In the past, you had to go to the editors directly and ask for a specific article, but now you can access the articles online in most cases. Unfortunately, they're not aggregated in a single database like you have in the States. Here, we have to go from one magazine's Web site to the next, one by one, or else spend days visiting libraries. We need information aggregators and more compilation of information in a single source—that's something I know we will see in the future.

Right now, there are a couple of big issues regarding international research. Customers feel they can get everything they need through the Internet. They think that the Internet can solve all their problems, and that's the only place they have to go to get information. We usually answer, "That's fine. But if you don't find it on the Internet, then call us and we will help you." What makes it hard is that North Americans are always talking about information availability. But, as I've said, we have very few databases in Spanish, and online governmental public information tends to be outdated. Sometimes you will find online access to public data, but it's two years old, and that does not help you if your business is to provide good information to your customer.

Another challenge we face when we are doing global research is trying to get current information from different countries. Sometimes, when you research Central American countries, you will find someone who offers to help you but says that it will take two or three months. They really do not care about timeliness. So you have to find another way of getting the data, because a customer cannot wait two months for the information.

It is very difficult to pull all the information together in the time frame that our customers give us. As a result, people tend to suspect, after you have spent all this time on their project and you have very few results, that you have not really done any work. I will say to them, "I had a researcher spend eight hours working to get you your information" and they say, "Yes, but you haven't given me anything that's valuable for me." It is hard for me to prove that somebody was actually involved in doing the project, when I don't have much to show them at the end because we couldn't get the information quickly enough.

To avoid this misunderstanding, what we often do is to run a preliminary research at no cost, no obligation for the prospect, to see what sources and information are going to be available. Then we make a proposal and explain what we can do. This has been great for reducing unreasonable expectations. We make sure to explain that we do not provide information; we provide research services. The proposal usually includes some useful information based on their requirements, and that is compelling for the prospect.

How easy is it to get information on companies in Latin America? Are the companies required to disclose much financial information?

It's hard. The information we get on companies tends to be from third parties—magazines, newspaper articles, etc. If the company goes public, it might be easier to get the balance sheet. But if the company is private, there's no way to get it unless you know somebody within the company, and even that does not guarantee anything. It's hard to find information in Latin America.

When we provide competitive intelligence research, we do what we can to find information, but then sometimes we need external tools to analyze the contents. Sometimes we have to get an economist or a professional to do the final analysis, to get the full picture of a specific company. On the other hand, we sometimes can fill in the gaps if we know somebody in the company. Since it is difficult to get internal information, we don't promise anything to a customer. We prefer to create low expectations at first; then if we get more complete information, the customer is happy. Of course, we never use any illegal or unethical means to get information about a company.

Do you have much of a problem with cultural blind spots? Are there times when a client asks a question that makes no sense in the local culture?

What I mentioned previously, regarding how we do preliminary research before we make a proposal, helps reduce this risk of cultural blind spots. When we run the preliminary research, we find the sources and basic data that we then include in the proposal. We can usually identify any problems or misunderstandings or unspoken assumptions before we start the real research. We start the project already having some background knowledge, since we've done some initial work. That's an entrepreneurial risk, of course, and sometimes we have not been able to get the contract after we invested a few days or a week of preliminary research, but it's the way we approach it, and it's proven to work with our business.

How do you stay up to date on new information sources?

The Internet is a tool for staying updated, and so is traveling to the States to attend conferences, and subscribing to a few magazines. The Internet is my main source for learning about what's new, what's updated, what's not being updated, new ventures, and new sites that provide local or regional information that might be interesting for my business purposes. I also have a few subscriptions to general-interest magazines, like *Business Week*, *Fortune*, and so on.

There aren't many email discussion lists in our region, so reading the online versions of newspapers in each country is basically how I stay updated about what's going on in terms of information availability, updates, and so on.

Do you use country- or region-specific search engines much?

We don't rely on them, because for most Latin American countries, only one or two search engines specific to that country exist, and their material often isn't updated frequently. We always need to double-check the sources and the data that we find through those search engines. We have local resources and contacts in each country, which we use to dig deeper. We want to cover the full spectrum of information sources, instead of just providing the customer with basic data. We want the customer to know that we provided thorough research, that we covered all the sources. You can't use the free search engines for that. We need to provide them with value-added service, because our customers can get into Yahoo! and do searches themselves, and we wouldn't exist if that was all they wanted.

Are there any free Web resources that you rely on?

There are a lot of free Web resources, but none of them is essential in our kind of business. I don't rely on free resources, though. In my experience, if a site is free, that means that the producer doesn't have as much incentive to provide balanced information or to keep the resource updated and well organized. And in the end, doing the research with free sources costs more, because of the amount of time required.

In terms of fee-based resources, we often go to the databases that contain the local magazines and the leading newspapers in each country. They often have very good collections of information, updated frequently, and often with photos as well as articles. Sometimes, we are able to contact the editors, and they can help us go back three or four years to get specific information. I should mention that we do not cover social sciences or medical research; we are focused on Latin American business information, so I have not looked at sources for those other areas.

How do you think international research is going to change over the next few years?

We will see more aggregator sites and partnerships among sources. I also think we will see more public information becoming available in the next two to five years. The regulatory environment will drive companies to become more open to the public and, as a result, more governments will open their own information to the public. The laws, regulations, and policies will push companies to open their information to the marketplace, and then more companies will be willing to be more transparent to the people.

Super Searcher Power Tips

➤ We become almost a partner with our clients, first understanding very clearly what they need the information for, and then helping them understand the context of the information we provide.

➤ Unfortunately, magazine and newspaper articles are not aggregated in a single database like you have in the States. We have to go from one magazine's Web site to the next, one by one.

➤ To avoid misunderstandings with clients, we often run a preliminary search to see what sources and information are going to be available. This has been great for reducing unreasonable expectations.

➤ If you need government information in Latin America, most of the time it has to be retrieved manually by someone located in the area. Forget about online research!

➤ In my experience, if a site is free, that means that the producer doesn't have as much incentive to provide balanced information or to keep the resource updated and well organized. In the end, doing the research with the free source costs more, because of the amount of time required.

Miranda van Roosmalen

Dutch Researcher and Trainer

Miranda van Roosmalen is Manager, Research and Library within the Knowledge and Research Centre at PricewaterhouseCoopers in Utrecht, the Netherlands. Her main tasks involve conducting research projects for consultants and writing industry analyses, both national and international.

miranda.van.roosmalen@nl.pwcglobal.com

Let's start with your background and how you started doing international research.

I've been a researcher now for some thirteen years. First I studied library and information science, then I started working for newspaper publishers in the research department, first at the local newspaper, *De Stem*—in English, *The Voice*—and after a year, at the national newspaper called *De Volkskrant*. I was partly a librarian and partly a researcher, and during the years I worked with *De Volkskrant*, I got involved more and more in research. I stayed there for about nine years, and then I decided that it was time for me to move on.

When you're doing research, you're always working for someone else. You're gathering information and that person is going to read the information and conduct an interview with someone, or write a profile on a company. So I thought, that's something I want to do myself. During that time, I learned what good desk research is all about. You need to be creative and flexible and persistent, because sometimes a person doesn't want to give you the information you are looking for. It also gives you a chance to get to know your sources and evaluate what are good sources and what aren't.

I started working at PricewaterhouseCoopers about three years ago, in a team of twelve researchers. As a senior researcher, I bring in new research projects from consultants within our firm. I do extensive research on companies, with a lot of international focus, because the companies we cover operate in the international environment. Even if the company or industry has a Dutch focus, we have to look internationally to see what the trends and developments are within the competitive environment.

Part of my job is to serve as a mentor for new researchers. We get a lot of people who have just graduated, and this is their first job. They want to do research and get to know an industry well, so part of my job is trying to coach them. I teach them the different phases of good desk research, starting with intake and asking questions to get the subject right, to conducting the research, making the selections, analysing the information, and putting it in a report that is pleasant to read.

Part of the Knowledge and Research Centre's job is to train business analysts, getting them to learn the sources and the industry. After two years, they become junior consultants within our company. Each year, five or six new colleagues come in, and we train them, and then they move on in the company. They're sort of ambassadors for us. They know the Knowledge and Research Centre and they know how to work with us on their projects.

It's great to be able to get all those people trained well at the beginning, so that they know how to use your services.

Yes, it's a win–win situation for everybody. The one disadvantage is that it's hard to do much knowledge management, because the junior consultants move around in the company so quickly. You have to make sure that the knowledge they have gathered is available for new colleagues as well.

I notice that you distinguish between librarians and researchers. What does a librarian do and what does a researcher do?

Here at the Knowledge and Research Centre, a librarian does quick reference questions: What's the phone number of a certain company? Can you give me an annual report of a company? What's been published the last three months on a particular subject? They are involved in keeping the library up to date, so they order books and they handle the magazine circulation within the company.

The researcher takes it a step further. Researchers are often dedicated to a particular industry. They are the contact people for the industry, so a consultant comes to them and says, "We're going to make a presentation, and I want you to make a few slides with data concerning country figures on gross domestic product and the inflation rate." So instead of just gathering information about a company as a librarian would, the researcher gathers the information, reads it, analyses it, puts the analysis in a report, and presents that to the consultant.

Can you describe a typical project? And what you would do, after gathering the information, to make it easier for the analyst to actually use it?

Once, I was involved in a project concerning energy service companies. They're in the utility sector; energy service companies help other companies or factories to reduce energy use. My job was to gather information about existing energy service companies—ESCOs, they're called. So, along with some of the project team members, I gathered information from the

Internet, talked to branch organisations [*Author's note: trade associations*], and gathered information on ESCOs in Northern Europe, Western Europe, Eastern Europe, and South Europe. The information I gathered was ten or fifteen centimetres high, and I had to distil it down to four pages. The other project members were consultants, and they were focused on the advising bit. They did some of the competitor analysis, but they knew they could rely on me to gather the information and to do the segment on the state of the art in the various regions. They read my part and they said, "Well, it's great." Those four pages went into the analyst's report, along with the critical success factors and the other advice we gave the client.

It is a great experience for me to work with consultants in projects, to attend all their meetings. When you're doing research, you're often working alone. When you're part of a team, you're working together on a project, and you can see how your job contributes to the final report. It's very stimulating, because you see all the ins and outs of the whole project.

Do you find that you approach research projects differently when you're looking for information in different regions of the world?

Well, the Internet is a very good source to start with nowadays, but once I'm there I might use different search engines to find the information. It's easy to put in a few descriptors and see what you get. If you don't get anything, then you can start to think about other options. In the project I just described, since we're part of Europe, we knew the sources to look at. For Latin America and Asia, it's hard to tell what resources the online databases contain, and when I do find something, it's usually in the wrong language. So I would first try to find people instead of information. I would start by contacting colleagues in other Knowledge and Research Centres within PricewaterhouseCoopers to see if they could gather information for me, because I'd expect a language difficulty with the sources. I mainly look for people who might give me names of organisations I could call, or companies they know of, the basics you need when you start searching.

When you start with an Internet search, do you go to one of the big search engines and just throw in some words, or do you go to a portal or a catalogue?

It depends on the question. If it's in one of my industries—right now, those are environment and waste, media and entertainment, and energy and utilities—I normally start with my bookmarks. I try to gather pages that have a lot of links to other pages. As a side note, I have to say that it's very important to build your own special subject library of "favourites" or bookmarks. It's one way I have of doing knowledge management. When I'm not in, someone else can get into my computer and look at my bookmarks and see the Internet pages I use frequently.

If it's a question on something I don't know much about yet, I will start with AltaVista [4, see Appendix]. There are so many search engines nowadays, I've decided that I'm going to use just two or three as a starting point. So it's AltaVista when I want to search the full text of Web pages; it's Yahoo! [160] when I need some hierarchy and selected web sites only. I use Copernic [202] when I think that a single search engine is not going to give me a lot of information, so I need to try a whole group of search engines at once.

Since you started at PricewaterhouseCoopers, what changes have you seen in the international information resources that are available for researchers?

One of the main things I've seen is that a lot more market research information is available digitally, so you don't have to depend on the opening hours of market research firms. You can search at the most convenient time for you without the necessity of already knowing exactly what you are looking for. You just start; you don't have to call anyone and say, "I'm looking for reports or information on this and this and this." So the availability of online market research has made the beginning of the research process easier. And you can buy parts of the report rather than the entire report. That's very important, because the amount you pay for the full report is very high. And some research firms even offer their information free.

I also think that FT.com [52] is great. With most newspapers and news sources that put their information online, you have to wait a day or so after publication for the information to appear on the site. FT.com puts the information on their Web site immediately, and you can build an alerting service so the information comes to you automatically. It's all much easier than it used to be. I've seen the research options grow and become more extensive than they used to be.

Another change I have seen is in the price structure. When searching international resources, you used to have to go in by modem, search with complicated techniques, and pay for the time you were in there. Now the options with various price structures give us more freedom to find the most convenient resource to use. If we use a source often, then we get a contract for a lump sum, or else we pay as we go.

What I've also seen in the fee-based information services like Dow Jones Interactive [35] is a growth in subject libraries made up of international resources. These help if you know generally what you're looking for, but you don't know the exact sources. You just select the appropriate subject library, and all the sources which contain information about that subject are in there, and you can search them all together.

One thing that annoys me is that among the large information providers, such as LexisNexis [88], DataStar [31], and Dow Jones Interactive, the coverage of the information is, in large part, similar to one another. LexisNexis has a few unique sources you absolutely need, so you have to have a subscription to them, and DataStar has a few other unique sources that you have to have.

So you can't just pick one, although sometimes I dream of one super online information source which contains all the sources I need. When I have contact with the vendors, sometimes I'll say that, and they look at me and say, "Yeah, yeah, we want that too, but ..." Then they start with their own marketing talk.

Are you noticing that more full-text information is being made available by government sources, or do you still have to go to a person within the government to get the full text of reports or papers?

The number of full-text reports from government agencies is increasing by the minute. The Dutch have an Internet site, Overheid.nl [106]. Overheid is Dutch for government. They put all sorts of free information there. Every ministry is on that site, and they have a search feature as well. That's great, because there is a lot of bureaucracy within the ministries, and if you don't have a name, it's very difficult sometimes to gather the information. They also give you links to the sites of corresponding ministries in other governments, at least within Europe.

There used to be such a great difference between the information you got from the U.S. ministries and from the European governments. Because I had seen how much was available from the U.S., my expectation was that everything was on the Internet. Sometimes it's very frustrating when you're looking for information on a specific subject, and all you get is information about the U.S. You think, "Well, that's great, but now I'm looking for the European focus or the Dutch focus." The Dutch ministries have taken large steps forward, but then the information is probably in Dutch, so that's a problem, too, if you can't read Dutch.

And, of course, there's the European Union site [45]. They have a search engine, and you can look up information, but you can't select a language when you search, and there are documents in eleven languages. So when you review your search results, you see the same article in Italian and in Greek and in English. You have to open each document, and then you see, oh, it's Italian, or it's Greek, and go to the next one. It is very frustrating. When you design such a database, you should ask yourself, "What do the users want? What's user-friendly?" I think the site designers just had so much information to deal with, and they said, "Well, we have to go electronically, so let's just dump it all in and put our backs against it and not listen to any of the comments."

One other trend I've noticed in international resources is that more and more companies publish external reports about their company on their own Web sites. I recently looked at the Web site of a company called Progress Software and discovered analyst reports about the company on their own site. That's a great trend for researchers. When you look for information about a company, if you first go to their official site on the Internet and can find all this external information, it can save you enormous amounts of time. Of course, I don't think you would find negative external reports on their own sites, but it's still useful to see what outside analysts are saying.

What is your biggest challenge in finding international information?

There are so many options when gathering information in these digital times, as I call them, that the enormous variety makes it hard to decide what is the best source for the information requested. And how do you know when you've found what you're looking for? It's very difficult to stop looking when you have been searching all day and not found any relevant information. Then you start to think, "Did I do my research to the best of my abilities; did I miss an important source; is there no information available on this subject, or can I just not find it?"

That's what I see with new researchers; they're not confident of their own ability to search. I tell them, "You've made a plan, you have a strategy, you've decided in cooperation with your co-workers on the best sources, you've searched them with the right descriptors. Be confident of your own abilities, and rely on your judgment."

I find it very difficult when I'm looking for information in a region for which I don't know many of the sources myself. I worry about whether I have missed something that would be obvious to someone in the country. Do you just trust your instincts, and figure that if you have developed a good strategy and haven't found much, then that must be the answer?

Yes, but I also ask co-workers. It's important to stop and reflect on your search up to that point. There comes a time when you think, "Well, I've done everything, and I still can't find what I'm looking for." Then you need someone at the other end of the table whom you can talk it over with. Brainstorming sometimes gives you another source that you would not have thought of otherwise. But sometimes you just have to keep track of what you've done, and if you can convince yourself that you've done everything to the best of your abilities to find the information within the time frame the consultants have given you, then you have to stop. I tell the consultant what I've done, why I've done it, and why I haven't come up with anything.

And sometimes, not finding anything is also an answer. You know, the consultant's core business is giving advice, and our core business is trying to get the information. When I'm conducting a search, my responsibility is to put in the effort to find the information. It's not my responsibility to find the information if it's not out there. Sometimes I hear colleagues say, "I've accepted this question, so I have to come up with information." I say, "How are you going to do that?"

Sometimes it's a matter of just not having enough hours to find the information. In that case, I can say to the consultant, "I've done these things, I haven't found it within this time frame, but I know it's out there. Give me a couple of hours more, and I will find it for you." For example, maybe you've found an abstract of a report on the Internet, and you think this might be something good, but there's not much information there, so you have to search in other sources to find the report, and that's going to take time. That's for the consultant to decide, based on the information you give him.

Once, when I was working at the newspaper, a new king was crowned in Belgium. In a speech, he made a reference to a book and its author, and a columnist at the newspaper was trying to find out just what the author had written. He knew what page he wanted, because that was mentioned in the speech. But he did not know what the author said exactly, and he wanted to use it in his column. I called the national library in Belgium and they said, "Yes, we have the book, but it's in the basement, and there's a person there but he doesn't have a phone." It was very difficult. So I faxed a request to the library, saying it was very important, and asked that someone give that person the fax with the request, if he came upstairs. After an hour or so, the guy called, and he said, "Yeah, I know what you are looking for. And what a coincidence—two months ago I gave this book to someone within the facility of the royal family." So I talked him into faxing me the two pages I needed. As it turns out, the font in the book was old, almost medieval, so it was very hard to read. We spent hours copying and enlarging it to make it readable. And when the column was published, there was a paragraph on the material that I had obtained. So I spent four or five hours just for one paragraph, but it was a fun project, and I felt that it was time well spent. Sometimes you just have to keep trying, and be persistent, even when you run into one obstacle after another.

What do you do when you are trying to find information and all the sources are in a language that you can't read?

That can be very hard. We have an international network within PricewaterhouseCoopers, so I often have co-workers who can help me. Sometimes I just get the article, and then try to find someone within my company who can translate it. If they're not available, I try to find publications that report about the region in English. For example, if I needed Asian sources, I might try to find information in *Asian Times,* which is in English. The international online databases sometimes have English abstracts for sources that are in other languages, so you can get an idea of what the article is about.

Another possibility is to use a search engine such as AltaVista's Babelfish [201], which translates sites into English. The translation isn't the best English, but it can give you an idea of the content, and sometimes it's just so much fun to see what it has done to the language. I've used Babelfish to see if there is anything on a site that might be relevant for me, and then I'll try to find someone who can translate it for me properly.

What I also might do, when the sources are in another language, is try to find a PricewaterhouseCoopers person within the country, and talk to him or her on the phone. Of course, sometimes that's a problem because that person doesn't speak English. But if it works, it's a good way to find some statistics or information about an industry.

A lot of times, research comes down to talking to people. That's one of the nice things about research. Instead of sitting behind your computer and looking at a screen, you can talk to people. I think it's a very important factor in doing international research.

A few years ago, we thought we could sit at our computers and type away and find everything we need. There seems to be more of a recognition now that you have to go out there and talk to the experts as well.

I think that knowledge management programs could be a help in this, because when you're talking to people, it's about the knowledge that is in their heads. If you could find a way to get that into writing or a database, that would help as well.

Do you run into any other challenges when you're doing international research?

Determining the reliability of the information is a challenge, primarily with information on the Internet, but also with online databases. How do you know that the information you find is reliable? Sometimes you're so pleased that you found any information at all that you forget to think about whether this is an official company Web page, or a page of a branch organisation, or whether it's from the government. It's something you always should keep in mind, because you're probably going to distribute the information to someone else or take it into account when making your analysis.

It is very frustrating, when I am trying to find information on a company, to find their Web site and want to call them, because the information I need isn't on the Internet, or I have a very specific question for someone—but I can't find an address or telephone number on the site. Sometimes I have had to go through twenty pages before I find a telephone number. I want to tell them, "Don't hide behind your site!"

Another frustration is when I've come so close to finding the report—I find an abstract on the Internet, I call the market research bureau to get a copy of it if it's not available online—and then they say, "We're going to send you an invoice by mail, and you have to pay first, and when we get your payment, we will send you the report by mail." But often I'm on a tight time schedule. I need the information within a week, so it's not going to work that way. It's so frustrating when they say, "No, no, this is the policy." It has gotten better lately, but the difference between getting information electronically and getting it by mail is so great. You know it's out there and you just can't get it in time. I'm so close—I can almost feel it, I can almost touch it—and at the same time it's so far away.

How do you stay up to date on new information sources?

For the Dutch environment, I subscribe to a magazine called *The Informatie Professional* [180]. It is a magazine in Dutch, published by Otto Cramwinkel Publisher. They have background articles on trends in the Netherlands, and all kinds of columns, and they list email and Web pages of organisations that have published reports. In the library here, we have an internal newsletter with tips and new Internet pages. Those are the main channels from which I get my information, along with just talking to colleagues. We have within PricewaterhouseCoopers a global knowledge management team, and each month ten or fifteen of us have a conference call. We inform each other about developments and suggestions for new sources. We also have a discussion database in which we can put questions such as "I'm looking for information on a subject; does anyone have suggestions?" or "I'm thinking about a contract with Information Vendor X; what are your experiences so far?"

What fee-based services and free Web services do you consider critical for international research? Which resources could you not live without?

The Web itself is essential. When you look at the Internet nowadays, you can't imagine the world without it. On the one hand, it's made our lives as researchers easier. On the other hand, it has made research more difficult because of the enormous amount of information available. For financial information or corporate information, I often use Hoover's [64] or CorporateInformation.com [27]. I often use government-based sites; for example, today I went to the *CIA World Factbook* [26] for information on countries, because it's so extensive. They have information on the economy, the population; they have every-thing! I go to FT.com, as I have said, because their archive with more than six million articles is on there for free. You can search the archive, and you can create a profile and they will send you updated information by email. They have industry surveys there, too. I think that's a great resource.

As I mentioned, I use the European Union site, because some-times you need information on Europe, and it's the best starting point. Once you get over all the language difficulties, you *can* find information there. I also use it for national statistics or for pointers to national sites. And I use Northern Light [100], because you can buy pages from extensive—and expensive—market research reports with a credit card.

I like using the World Bank [153] site because now it lets you make your own tables of selected countries for a search. Other sites will have a grouping called Eastern Europe or Western Europe, but you might want Eastern Europe plus three other countries, for example. And I always try to find a single source when I am looking for factual or statistical information, so that the numbers are comparable, and I like using the World Bank for that kind of research.

As for the fee-based services, we use Dow Jones Interactive a lot for news, partly because we have a global contract with them. It's very user friendly. It has loads of information, and it's just great to search the full text of 6,000 sources at one time, or to be able to search very specific sources for particularly news. I also use Nexis [98], DataStar, and Profound [111].

What trends do you see in global research?

I think the availability of personal agents will increase, so when you're doing an alerting service on a specific subject, the technol-ogy will do more and you can focus more on the actual research and analysis. I also see, for instance, AltaVista going back to being a portal and not being involved in e-commerce activities, because they see that the market is asking for efficient and user-friendly ways to find your way through all the information on the

Net. A lot of search sites will focus more on the search options, and not on the additional things they have been doing.

As for the international online databases, I think there will be fewer in the future, because a large portion of the information is similar among the various competitors. The specialised databases will increase, because nowadays more and more industry sectors are getting used to the Internet and to e-business, so there will be more of a demand for information on specific subjects. That's something the market will respond to.

If I think back seven or eight years at how I did research then, versus how it's done now, the difference is unimaginable. Back then, you might remember that you had read an article in the paper copy of the newspaper several weeks ago, so you would have to start browsing through the back issues. Worse yet, you might have to contact the publisher and find out if they have an archive, and if so, whether they can provide you with an article if you provide them with the date and the title. At the end of the day, you might have found four or five articles. Now it's so much easier to get information.

Super Searcher Power Tips

➤ When researching in a region that I'm not familiar with, I would first try to find people instead of information. International research often comes down to talking to people, instead of sitting behind your computer and looking at a screen.

➤ Building your own special subject library of "favourites" or bookmarks is one way of doing knowledge management.

➤ I use AltaVista to search the full text of Web pages, Yahoo! when I need some hierarchy and selected Web sites only. I use Copernic when I think I need to try a whole group of search engines at once.

➤ FT.com puts news sources on their Web site immediately, and you can build an alerting service so the information comes to you automatically.

➤ Sometimes you're so pleased that you found any information at all that you forget to think about whether this is an official company Web page, or a page of a branch organisation, or whether it's from the government.

Christine Windheuser

Information on the Developing World

Christine Windheuser is the Special Projects Librarian at the World Bank/International Monetary Fund Library Network in Washington, DC. Her work focuses on creating new electronic products for the Library Network to deliver to clients via email and intranets.

cwindheuser@worldbank.org
jolis.worldbankimflib.org/external.htm

First, can you tell me about your background?

I have a BA and an MLS from the University of Wisconsin and have been with the World Bank for twenty-two years. As you probably know, the World Bank is a development institution that focuses on international development, aid loans, and technical assistance to the developing world. Prior to becoming the Special Projects Librarian, I was the head of public services at the World Bank's Sectoral and IT Resource Center.

How much of your work focuses on international research?

Currently, my work focuses on product development rather than reference and research. However, in my former position—until January 2000—I supervised research staff. All our work is focused on information about the developing countries to which the World Bank lends, although we also include comparative material from the industrialized world. The section of the World Bank/IMF Library Network in which I work, the Sectoral and IT Resource Center, handles technical questions about major sectors of the economy in which the World Bank lends. These include agriculture, education, energy, environment, health, nutrition, population, rural and urban development, transportation, telecommunications and IT, mining, water supply, and gender issues. Our clients are subject specialists on the World Bank staff who are working on lending programs and technical assistance in these areas.

Can you describe a typical international research project that you get at the World Bank?

Someone at our resident mission in Indonesia who's working with the government there on hospital improvement sends us an email asking us for information about hospital accreditation systems around the world, because the Indonesians either don't have one or theirs doesn't work well. We would do a literature search for useful material and, because we're using the Internet as a heavy production tool, we're going to look not only at the academic literature but for actual Internet sites, such as an international hospital accreditation association or full-text Internet documents on the topic. We'll email a response based on a template that says, "Dear so-and-so, here's your literature search with relevant Internet sites." Because we've got electronic licenses for a lot of journals, we try to include the direct URL to the article; that way, the person who's in Indonesia doesn't have to write back to us and say, "Yes, please print these articles and send them to Indonesia via inter-office pouch." All they have to do is click on the URLs, open the articles from our article suppliers, and print them at their site.

That's a typical interaction where the person asks a question and we look at a lot of different sources, both traditional online sources and the Internet directly. We repackage the material in a template, and we email it to them so that they can get the answer right at their desk. That's the ideal situation. The less-than-ideal situation is when they're far away and we have to print the items out in hard copy and mail them to the clients; that's not always satisfactory because the international pouch system can take five to six days.

When you're looking for original source documents on the Net, how do you locate PDF or Word files, or anything else that's not plain HTML?

Well, in the old days when you had one good article and you wanted to find related items, you would see who cited that article; that's just old-fashioned citation searching. Now, we use the concept of what I would call *site pearling*. First, you find a site that's relevant. Most sites have a "related links" area, which lets you expand your reach; in some of these sites you're going to find links to items that are fairly relevant. The idea is that you start with a small pearl and then you build upon it.

In a direct search, I usually use AltaVista [4, see Appendix], which is really good at looking for specific items. It will take you right down to the document level on a site. Sometimes I can find the item that way. And now that Google [59] searches for PDF files when you add "filetype:pdf" to your search, it's a little easier to find some of that hidden information.

That's a great tip. I also like the reverse Web link look-up technique, where you find one killer site and use Google or AltaVista to see who's linking to that site. So, what changes have you seen in international research resources over the past couple of years?

The move from paper to electronic digital availability has been the most important trend. Reference books, statistics, and major international serial text publications in digital format have allowed us to construct intranet-based subject pathfinders for our clients, and to create customized sections of our corporate intranet personalized down to the subject sector.

E-journal services and electronic table of contents services help us keep clients up to date in their fields and reduce our document delivery overhead. And major digital information services for country information like the EIU [37], ISI Emerging Markets [78] and Oxford Analytica [107], have allowed us to put resources on every staff member's computer desktop and to create customized sections of our corporate intranet personalized down to the country level.

Can you tell me more about the intranet-based pathfinders?

You remember the concept of pathfinders in the old days, when they were paper lists of your favorite reference sources? Well, our pathfinders are similar, but instead of directing clients to paper sources, we're looking for Internet versions of those sources, or we're pointing to sources that don't exist except on the Internet. It's as if we took a paper pathfinder and converted it to the Web world.

In our organization, we've divided up knowledge into twenty-one sectors, such as energy, the environment, health, water resources, international economics, and so on, and each reference librarian focuses on a few of these sectors and develops pathfinders on the intranet. Each pathfinder has a set of preset catalog searches on themes within that subject. It also has a set of suggested databases that people should use for searching on that subject. And we include a set of statistical sources, referring people to both printed sources and Internet resources. We'll include a list of core organizations in that sector, and sites we think are useful but that we can't shoehorn into any of our pre-formatted categories.

We get a lot of summer interns, and often we want to steer them to the pathfinders rather than actually do a lot of research for them. It's their job to learn to do research, so we show them the tools. For a senior person, of course, we do the research ourselves.

We keep the pathfinders up to date by running a link-checker every month, which parses out the broken links and reports them to whoever is maintaining that pathfinder. And, of course, everyone is expected to be looking out for new sites and for sites that need to be updated.

What's the hardest part of doing international research?

Because our focus is the developing world, the actual availability of data or information is the main problem. Sometimes the information exists, but only in the gray literature of other international organizations or aid agencies. So we have become experts in knowing what other UN, multilateral, and bilateral organizations have to offer. Gray literature is an area that people overlook; each organization has its own publishing or production area, and standard search tools aren't going into the databases of these other organizations and capturing what I would call the document-level items. Usually people can figure out the organization's URL just by looking at its acronym—for instance, the International Labour Organization will be www.ilo.org. It's essential that people remember that they're not going to capture all the information with a standard literature search—they have to go directly to the Web site of the relevant organizations.

I suppose the problem also exists in the professional online services; they don't capture the gray literature either, do they?

It depends. I would say that you can't rely on any one source anymore to provide a complete view. Since you can now go much more deeply into organizations' products and catalogs on the Internet, you can't just stop with standard online sources. You have to think carefully about whether you need to go directly to the producer's Web site. And that really is a good habit to get into, because you always get the most current material.

Do you find that cultural blind spots—unspoken assumptions about what information will be available, how it will be presented, or where it will be published—are much of a problem?

Sometimes our clients ask for data that no one in the country, or at an international agency, is mandated to collect. For data to be available, there must be programs to create it. In many developing countries they can hardly collect the most basic statistics. In fact, the World Bank has a lending program to help member countries set up statistics systems that will help collect the data they need for proper decision making.

How do you handle the difficulty of using sources or search tools that aren't in a language in which you're fluent?

We have staff who are fluent readers of French, Spanish, Russian, German, and Chinese. I can read German and Spanish, and after twenty-two years have somehow absorbed "French for Reading" by osmosis!

However, a key shortcoming is that most of the major online search services we use only cover English-language sources. That bias in the content is a concern. That's why the Library Network subscribes to services like ISI Emerging Markets that focus on local news sources and help to balance our business/economics sources.

We do get a fair number of non-English resources through Reuters Business Briefing [115]. We're feeding this into our organization via a service called Newsmachine, which is software from

Sagemaker [116] through which you can pipe all kinds of news and any kind of fielded data that can be broken down and analyzed. It has a search interface that isn't great, but good enough.

We also use a lot of specific bookmarks to individual newspapers. We're building pages on our catalog for electronic newspapers. We're finding the direct URLs for overseas newspapers, which is fairly easy to do. There are lots of different sources for that information, but my favorite is The Ultimate Collection of News Links [138]. We're making a catalog record for each of those items, and then we have a procedure whereby we dynamically call up all the items into a template we've made that sorts them out by country. We've done the same thing for our journals, but that was a little easier because we just had to go from A to Z, then by subject. So we're creating dynamic aggregates of newspaper entries for our catalog.

Do you use any country-specific Web search engines?

There are a few that we use. WorldSkip [156] is one, and Orientation.com [104]. They both have a very geographical focus, and let you search Web sites and news stories by country or region. We license a lot of country-level information from sources like EIU and ISI. Mostly, we're looking at an industry or subject, so we'll often approach a project from a subject point of view. Let's say we were doing research on the health sector; we would go to the National Library of Medicine's HealthSTAR [62] database as opposed to just going to some general resource on a country and hoping to find some health information there. We have to have an authoritative source, and that's usually subject-based rather than country-based.

That said, we *do* have a specialized bookmark set of over 1,500 sources for the subject sectors we support. One of the best of the best among those bookmarks is Governments on the WWW [61]. It is divided up by region, and then has selections for individual countries. It has URLs for individual government departments, and it's particularly good for somebody who's working at a real detailed level within a country.

InternationalAffairs.com [76] is a free site created by the consulting firm Oxford Analytica, and it's one of our favorite resources. It includes resources that the consulting firm uses in its work, and it's really a handy source. It's divided by region rather than by individual countries, which we find very useful. We also use the U.S. Department of State [145] Country Commercial Guides, which are annual guides to doing business in an individual country. They look at the commercial environment and provide some economic, political, and market analysis.

We also use ELDIS [39], from the Institute of Development Studies at the University of Sussex; it's the world's largest development information database. What they've done is captured specific documents and information from organizations' sites and mounted all of that in a searchable database. ELDIS is a really good one-stop place for information about international development activities in developing countries. And finally, we use Government Information on the Internet [60].

And what fee-based online sources do you consider essential?

Let's start with the Economist Intelligence Unit. EIU provides country and country risk analysis—spin-offs of their original paper productions, which came out both annually and quarterly. They're detailed and they have a lot of statistical data, which you can then export into a spreadsheet in case you want to do some further reanalysis of the data. It's different from a news service in that it's not real-time news, but it gives you an analysis of an issue, what the issue means, and what its possible ramifications might be. It's very, very useful if you're looking for information on the impact of a recent event.

ISI Emerging Markets is a company that deals with news, company information, and financial data from twenty-eight emerging market countries in Europe, Latin America, and Asia.

We also use Reuters Business Briefing, which we rely on more for real-time news from around the world. Dow Jones Interactive [35] is good for news and full-text publications. We use LexisNexis [88] for full-text news searches. And, of course, we use Dialog [33] as well, mainly for faster staff access to many of the databases that we also license for desktop use by our organization. We can work more quickly in Dialog's command mode so we dial in directly rather than using the desktop access.

What do you find particularly challenging when doing global research?

The thing that really drives us crazy is the number of mergers and acquisitions among the online information vendors. When we're trying to buy or license online resources, either for ourselves or to provide to our clients, it always feels like such a moving target. At times, we've made decisions based on the way things were, and then the next week they've changed. For instance, when we went to license a news source, back before Dow Jones Interactive and Reuters formed Factiva [48], we were in a quandary. We wanted to be able to get access to the *Financial Times* and the Reuters information products, but we preferred the interface of Dow Jones Interactive. So we settled on a third option, with Sagemaker, which offered more of a build-your-own interface. Now, of course, the Dow Jones people are in bed with the Reuters people. We wish we'd known that the joint venture was coming and that we could have had a third option.

On top of that, the vendors continue to feed data to other aggregators, but they embargo the news for a certain amount of time, so if you want the latest news, you have to go directly to the publisher. It's such a moving target!

How do you know when you've done a thorough search and it's time to quit?

We have a template that we use, which reminds us to ask ourselves, "Did I look in the catalog, did I look in external sources, did I look at Internet sites?" You have to remember to look in all three of those areas to make sure you've found the information that will satisfy the client. At the top of the template, we list what sources we went to.

We don't put just anything into the final report. We want to review the results and cull out the items that don't seem to be all that focused. People only want material that is the most relevant and most recent. So by considering those two areas—relevance and timeliness—we're usually able to reduce the amount of excess that we send to the client.

What trends do you see in doing international research? How do you think research will be different in a couple of years from what you're doing now?

The general trend is toward personalization. In our intranet work, we've been able to create pages that are customized—not to the client/desktop level, but to the country level. In other words, we can cut up information sources and show sources by country, but we haven't reached the point where we're able to have clients see just the parts of our intranet that they choose. But I think there will be more and more ability to personalize services at the individual level, and we'll be spending more time helping people set up their personal profiles so they're getting just the little snippets of things that they want. Right now we can only do it down to the broad level. If you're interested in the subject of health, you get everything on health. But we're moving toward greater and greater individual personalization.

The thing is, we're at the point where people are almost saturated by information. People don't want entire sources any more; they want just portions of sources that are relevant to them, which can be very tricky to provide. In our work on the newsfeed service, we've gotten to the point where we can create personalized profiles, but the problem is that the more narrowly you filter, the more relevant items you lose. You can narrow your search down, but you might miss something useful. It all comes back to precision versus recall.

Do most of your clients need the same type of information all the time, so that an alerting service would make sense? Or do most of your research projects involve one-off questions?

Many of our clients are working on fairly long-term projects with our member governments. So they probably want to know about certain things on an ongoing basis. We have a table of contents service, but we can't personalize it to the individual client level, because that would be too labor intensive. For instance, for the health sector, we divide the tables of contents into health, population, and nutrition, and that's really as far as we can go economically. We distribute that table of contents, and the clients pick out the articles that they want. Ideally, we would set up individual profiles for everyone, help them select the search terms, and deliver only the tables of contents that contain the phrases that are of interest to them. Unfortunately, organizational budgeting comes into play here. We aren't able to charge everyone a set fee that would cover the costs for this personalization. Instead, we have to say to them, "If you would like this to be more personalized, you can charge the cost to your corporate credit card." Money often drives the choices you can offer.

On the other hand, it does give us a negotiating tool. There have been situations in which we've said, "If you want this specific item, you'll have to give us this much money." In some cases, they've ponied up. But in many cases, it's too much trouble and they just go away. So we see a lot of negative aspects to the fee-based approach. When they see a price tag, they get scared.

What percentage of your journals do you get in electronic format?

About 45 percent of our journals are delivered electronically. Most of those are tied to our having a paper subscription as well. But we're going through a program now in which we're converting a lot of our paper subscriptions to electronic-only, particularly those publications that most people don't browse in the library. They'll only exist in the library catalog with a URL, and that's going to save us a good bit of space. But for many subscriptions, we can't cancel the paper copy because either the electronic version is tied to the paper subscription, or people like to look at the paper copy. For example, *Lancet* is a very popular journal, and we have both electronic access and paper access, but people like to be able to come in and just skim through the hard copy.

How do you keep track of bookmarks to useful Web sites?

Over the years, we've found many, many useful sites. So, rather than waste all that work, we've recycled some of those into pathfinders. But we've also begun building an entire set of bookmarks that cover the various sectors within the World Bank. We keep these on our reference terminal and on our public workstations. So if we're working with a client, we can say, "Here are some sites that you should really take a look at." We don't have to remember the addresses of these items; we just go to the bookmark file. We encourage the clients to make copies of the bookmarks and take them to their desks.

The problem is that our bookmark file has gotten so large that we can no longer put it on our internal shared drives. We have close to 1,500 sites now, which makes for a huge file. Some day we'll figure out how to get all of that onto everyone's desktop.

Super Searcher Power Tips

➤ Use "site pearling": find a highly relevant site on the Internet, go to its "Related Links" section, and look for related pearls further down in the information chain.

➤ My favorite site for finding the direct URLs for overseas newspapers is The Ultimate Collection of News Links.

➤ Sometimes the information exists, but only in the gray literature of international organizations or agencies. You have to become an expert in knowing what organizations have to offer. Gray literature is an area that people overlook.

➤ You have to remember that you're not going to capture all the information in a standard literature search; you have to go directly to the Web site of the relevant organizations.

Left to right: Vicky Connor, Geraldine Clement-Stoneham, Cris Kinghorn, and Teresa St. Clair.

Cris Kinghorn and Colleagues

International Banking Brain Trust

This was a group interview with Super Searchers from the London office of Deutsche Bank AG. Participants include Cris Kinghorn (CK), Director, Business Information Services, Europe and Africa; Vicky Connor (VC), Research Manager; Geraldine Clement-Stoneham (GCS), Researcher Manager; Kristin Michie (KM), Research Coordinator; and Teresa St. Clair (TSC), Researcher.

cris.kinghorn@db.com

Let's go around the table and have each of you tell me a little about your background.

CK: I'm actually not a librarian. When I was a child, I wanted to be a librarian, probably because I thought that then I would be allowed to take out more than the two books allowed each day from the children's library! I have a business degree with marketing, and I started my working life as a researcher, initially within television, then in advertising agencies. After that, I had about six months doing consultancy, then I was approached by a contact here in London to see whether I was interested in setting up an information centre at the corporate finance unit of Citibank. I initially approached this as another consultancy role, but at the end of the second week they asked me if I would accept a permanent job there. I found it to be gut-wrenchingly different from my previous experience in advertising; huge levels of stress are created when your mouth is saying, "Fine, leave it with me, I'll see what I can find," and your brain is thinking, "What the hell are they asking for?" Every industry has its own acronyms, but investment banking is an entirely different language.

I was at Citibank for six years altogether, then about five years ago, Carol Ginsburg approached me about moving over to Banker's Trust, which has since become part of Deutsche Bank. When the two banks were integrating and the structure of Business Information Services was being created and new roles defined, Carol used to jokingly refer to me as the Empress of all Europe—unfortunately bank communication standards don't allow me to put that on my business cards!

VC: I have been a researcher since graduating in 1990. My first job was as a graduate trainee in an academic library. After a year I moved over to the business world and worked for a management consultancy and as sole Information Officer for a firm of Chartered Accountants. I joined Deutsche Bank in 1997. I have been researching global information for more than eight years.

GCS: I graduated in 1997 and entered the corporate finance information world at Bankers Trust here in London in 1998. I have been doing global research since I started here.

KM: I graduated in 1995 and I worked at a consultancy before Deutsche Bank. I've been at Deutsche Bank for three years, so I've been doing global research for about five years.

TSC: I graduated in 1997 and I've been working in the banking sector for the last couple of years.

Do you get calls from all over the world, or just from the U.K.?

CK: From the management perspective, because we are part of a global network, we do try to support each other's user communities where this is practical. Some investment banks have a formal method of handing off requests as one location closes, so that they offer a "follow the sun" service. We don't do it in quite that way, but we do try to act as a network and support bankers anywhere on the globe when their local support is not available for whatever reason. We are feeling pressure to provide support for longer periods of time. We have a shift which works until midnight, so London is only down eight hours out of every twenty-four, Monday to Friday. Increasing desktop access enables bankers to be largely self-sufficient at the weekend, although support can be provided on request. We regularly find requests from Asia waiting for our attention each morning. And inevitably, some bankers here will request information from our New York office if they've got a really urgent request and it's past midnight here.

The bankers have to have the comfort level of knowing that they can get an answer to their question when they need it— whatever time that is in relation to their local business day. Carol Ginsburg would love to eventually have one telephone number for BIS around the world. The banker should neither know nor care where his request is being serviced; he should have complete confidence that the work will be done professionally in a cost-effective manner and within his turnaround time. I think that would be an ideal situation, but realistically, we're still some way off from that. There are some internal issues which hinder our achieving this kind of support—cross-border cost reallocation, for example .

Do you find it hard juggling time zones? Are there occasions when you can't speak with the banker because you're twelve hours apart?

CK: We can usually speak to the requesting banker because they keep such insane hours. When we find requests from a banker on the other side of the world we can see by the way the email is phrased that, even though it's way past midnight for him, he is not going to go home until we send him what he needs. It's interesting; I attended a presentation about providing global service, and the consensus from the participants, who were from a variety of global Wall Street firms, was that the most critical issue is also the most simple—that of "time." It's a fact of life today that, when their geographic location would lead you to the assumption that bankers would be in bed, they're all too frequently still working, and if they work for a global organisation they expect global support. BIS has a number of regular conference calls on a variety of topics, and inevitably at least two participants will be calling in from home in their pyjamas—someone's just got out of bed and someone else is just about to get in. If you're not prepared to deal with that, then you'll find it hard to be effective in this kind of environment. I'm now so used to it that I don't really think about it anymore.

Can you describe a typical global research project?

VC: It is difficult to define a typical request, as we get asked for so many diverse things. We get research projects on industries, companies, and markets. Many of the global requests we get can be for overviews of a given industry—major players, market shares, current trends, forecasts of what will happen in five years, projections of earnings, etc. Other requests can be for economic research—forecasts of GDP, demographics, and currency forecasts, for example. In addition, we spent much of our time creating global league tables of investment banks' performance, by product or industry or geography, for other areas of the Bank.

GCS: We usually start the research by looking at our own sources. We have access to loads of online databases, and we would probably start with a review of what market research has been produced. The next step would be to look up the relevant trade associations to see if they have a web site. For the leisure industry, for example, we would look for a leisure association. Then we would probably look for market research, industry journals, do a more global Internet search, and finally, go on one of the professional online services and do a global search of articles.

How do you evaluate the validity of sources that are outside the U.K.?

VC: We will often call our counterparts in the appropriate country and ask for their recommendations for an authoritative source. It can be very difficult, especially when you're looking at material on the Internet, because you don't know when the information was updated, whether it is still current, whether there is a better source. Sometimes it is just a matter of doing research over and over and over, trying to find other sources so you can draw comparisons among them. We look for a consistent story across sources. But even so, it's difficult. For example, if we were comparing Europe and the U.K., the data may be expressed in euros in some countries and in the local currency in others; or we might find forecasts for one country but statistics from 1995 in another country. It's always very difficult to draw absolute comparisons.

Do you find it difficult to manage the expectations of your clients, since they may be accustomed to getting consistent information from U.K. sources?

KM: That is one of the problems we have with doing global research; sometimes it's not possible to get everything from one source, so we do have to explain to them that this is the best information available, even thought it's not completely consistent.

VC: Quite often, we start with something like the Organisation for Economic Co-operation and Development [103, see Appendix], so at least you know that the data is being collected consistently. And we use the major Web sites like the EU's Europa site [45]. Once you've found top-level European data and top-level U.S. data, the banker is going to expect to be able to get the same from eastern European. Unfortunately, that is not always the case. Quite often, even though bankers want global research, they will settle for the U.S. and Western Europe. Junior bankers often expect you to find them all the data they want, while the more experienced banker will know that this kind of data is very difficult to gather.

What do you do when you're looking for information outside the regions that you're familiar with?

KM: That's the advantage of working for a global company; we've got colleagues in most regions. If we're unsure of where to go, or if there's a problem with the time difference, we can always contact one of our colleagues in Tokyo or Brazil. They're very good about getting back either with the information that we need or with pointers to where we need to go to get the information.

What changes have you seen in international information resources over the last few years?

VC: A few years ago, information on U.S. markets would be easy to find on the Internet. That was fantastic when you needed U.S. information, but you could get virtually nothing for Europe and certainly couldn't find information on markets beyond Europe. It's slowly changing, and Europe is catching up with the U.S. We are at the stage now where we can start to expect to get information on the Middle East and Eastern Europe the same ways you could on Western Europe five years ago. There are still problems with the quality of the data, though, and how up to date it is, but it is a start.

At the same time that free information is more readily sourced, information from paid sources seems to have become less readily available. Research reports that we get from databases like Profound [111] are not as easily available as they were in the past. You used to be able to get really good pan-European reports and global reports. Maybe the vendors have wised up a bit and are now removing their really good reports from host databases and making us go to them directly. So, it's getting better and it's getting worse.

It seems that instead of being able to access one database and download a variety of tables of contents for bankers, or get them one really good chapter or table for £10 or £20, you have to purchase bigger sections, which are priced accordingly.

What do you find most difficult about doing international research?

KM: I think the biggest challenge is not being able to get all the information from one single source. The inconsistency of data is an issue if we're doing sector research and gathering information from different countries. The other issue is language. Not everything is in English, and we don't always have someone available who speaks the language we need.

VC: Actually, lots of the bankers speak the languages that we don't. We have a Scandinavian team, and they will want information on Scandinavia, so often our role will be to find them URLs and let them contact the organisations directly, since none of us speak any Scandinavian language. We would do the next step if we could, but it is not always the best use of our or the banker's time.

GCS: We have found a couple of Web sites that allow you to put in the URL and then get a rough translation of the site, although we're having some technical problems getting through the Deutsche Bank firewall to actually get to these sites. That's another problem we encounter in doing research—the technical aspects. Often, we either are not allowed to access the site or it doesn't work.

VC: In terms of free Web translation sites, we use Babelfish [201] and FreeTranslation.com [203], although, as Geraldine said, we are having problems with our firewall for both these services.

Another problem we encounter is that, when we're looking for information, it can be difficult to know if the source is biased. Are the trade associations funded in a certain way? If you're looking for information on motor vehicles, are the sources funded by the car manufacturers? Where does the data come from? We try to get as many sources as possible so we can make some comparisons and make sure that one bit of data isn't wildly different from another bit. If the data is very hard to come by, and if we have the time, we sometimes commission market research agencies and independent information professionals to research and compile the information on behalf of the banker.

Do you run into many problems with legal restrictions on moving information across country borders?

KM: We do run into a bit of that. If there are copyright issues, we try to explain the situation to the banker and offer an alternative way of getting information, perhaps by going to a Deutsche Bank information centre in the banker's country, or in the country where the information originates, depending on the situation. We run into situations where the banker is asking for a prospectus from a country that doesn't allow the filings to be distributed outside the country. Again, we have to explain the problem and the legal implications, and try to offer alternative solutions. This kind of situation doesn't happen all the time; maybe once or twice a year.

VC: I had that happen to me recently. I accessed a German company's Web site and wanted to download a prospectus. I was prompted to enter a German postal code and address in order to get the document, since this was only available to people living in Germany. I would never try to make up an address, so I had to go back to the banker and explain why I couldn't get the information.

CK: The Bank will always take the stand that we never knowingly or deliberately breach copyrights. But copyright is very difficult to control in an organisation this size; it's a nightmare to manage well. We certainly try; we do everything that we can in countries where there is copyright legislation, a copyright clearance bureau, or any other similar arrangement. We make sure that we're licensed everywhere that we can be, in order to do as much as we might want to do, but always within the letter of the law.

Realistically, an agency may be the copyright licensing authority for that particular country, but it may actually be pretty toothless. A lot of publishers deliberately elect to stay out of the copyright agency for their country; they won't make their publications part of those agreements. When we have a circumstance like that, we will negotiate separately with the publisher if they provide critical data for the bank. We have in the past set up independent copyright clearance agreements with specific publishers. And we make it very clear to all of our employees what the policy is.

Can you talk a little more about issues regarding negotiating global licenses with vendors?

CK: BIS is very fortunate to have a global vendor relationship manager. He lives in New York and comes over regularly to review U.K.- or European-specific contracts. With us, the real burning issue over the last twelve months has been the integration of contracts. When Bankers Trust and Deutsche Bank came together, duplicate data was being delivered all over the place. It's very time-consuming to resolve these issues. You think that you've finally got everything nailed, and then a user pops up with a training issue, say, and you realize that you didn't catch all the contracts yet.

We handle contracts for products and services that are used both by the BIS researchers and on the banker's desktop. Managing desktop content has become an increasingly important part of what we do, and a critical use of our content expertise. I have staff who are now dedicated to supporting only that function. In fact, a former researcher is now my desktop product manager, and she has a team who work on the administration issues associated with this—processing and reallocating the invoices, making sure the users know the cost of the product, getting appropriate levels of sign-off so that we have an electronic trail of authorisation and technical permissioning—in fact, managing all of the technological aspects of each product and, on installation, the end-user training programme.

We try to enforce a "no training, no access" rule, but investment bankers can be very slippery to pin down. Most of this process will shortly be facilitated via the BIS Web pages, which will streamline the process considerably. The bank probably has over 200 individual products and services that get delivered to end users. BIS London currently manages over one hundred of those; it varies considerably city to city. If you look at the detail of that list, you'll see that some products have four users, and some have many hundreds.

Of course, we're selective in what information is made available around the world. When we deal with a global contract, we won't have global desktop access for a U.K.-based vendor that is providing a U.K.-focused product. Each BIS has the standard selection of resources—LexisNexis [88], Dow Jones Interactive [35], and so on—but every BIS will also have resources which are geographically specific. It makes no sense for us to be trained and stay proficient in a source that is only useful for the people in Hong Kong, for example. And the office in Johannesburg may be less interested in global contracts because the amount of South African-specific information that any vendor provides is actually relatively small. So, unless it's really going to be very, very cheap, it makes no sense for them to be part of that deal.

Do you have a list of the service issues that are critical for global contracts with online vendors?

CK: All vendors are increasingly realising that there's global business to be had, but they have to be able to service it correctly. Vendors that are inflexible and intransigent find that they lose their business with us, because this is a very competitive marketplace. If we can't get appropriate pricing, which is all the more important for a product which hopes to be on many hundreds of desktops, or we can't get the vendor to listen to how we need to have the product delivered, it's very hard for us to make a case to use them.

For example, invoicing is very important because, although we are a global bank, there are often country-specific tax issues that have to be considered. So we are increasingly pushing the responsibility of invoicing on a country-by-country basis back to the vendor. And the vendor who says, "Well, we're going to have to employ someone to do that for you, and we will want to charge you for that," is a vendor who will find the value of their relationship with us declining. Most now realise that, for whatever we need them to do, it's important that they find a way of doing it. They accept that we have service issues above and beyond providing a good product with good content and good functionality that is useful to the researchers. There are a whole raft of other issues that come with increasing desktop access.

I think the key to all of this is for the vendor to be flexible, to listen, and then to work with us to do what they can, even if it means putting themselves out a little bit. It's not just invoicing a certain location, it's making sure they invoice the correct location, putting the correct legal entity on the invoice, having a very good eye for detail. And if we go back to them six months into the contract and say, "You know this wonderful system that we have set up? Well, we need to change it," the vendor should not groan, or at least not until after they put the phone down! I do have sympathy with our vendors, because we're definitely a very hard taskmaster in a lot of respects. But for some of them, we are their single largest client, so they recognise the wisdom of keeping us happy.

Do you often run into cultural blind spots, where the banker presupposes that certain information will be available based on assumptions about other cultures?

GCS: We do come across this sort of situation fairly often. One of the most common situations is when we look for company accounts. The rules for filing accounts are very different from one European country to the next. Someone who's used to the U.K. market and how much information we can find on every company, private and public, would often assume that this is possible in other European countries, but it's not the case. Our bankers sometimes find it difficult to understand that, no, we can't access certain documents because the filing requirements are different.

Another expectation that I often come across is about free information. Everything should be free, whether it's statistics or market research. Quite a few of the new bankers don't understand that there is actually a cost involved in most cases. They have the assumption that we access everything on the Internet and that everything will be there and it will all be free.

VC: Also, a lot of them have used very well-funded university libraries, in which the vendors have put their databases at no charge to the students. Bankers are used to being able to spend hours searching, pulling down anything they want without charge. When they come to us and we say to them, "Okay, we're going to charge you X amount per month to have this database," it can shock them, because they are used to having everything at their fingertips for nothing.

Going back to something else Geraldine was saying, I think that the bankers who have mostly worked on U.S. companies, and are used to the U.S. Securities & Exchange Commission filings for

10Ks and 10Qs, find it difficult to come to terms with the differences in filing requirements in Europe. Over here, if you get an annual report for an Italian company, you'll be lucky to get it in English, and you'll be lucky to get it within eighteen months of the filing date. That has caused problems when people try to compare companies. The reverse happens with European bankers; they're used to being able to get information on private European companies, and they are surprised at how little we can get from private U.S. companies. Until all the legal bodies get their acts together and say, "This is what you need to file if you are a private company," we're always going to have those problems.

How do you manage the bankers' expectations in this regard?

VC: When they join the bank, all new bankers have BIS training as an integral part of their general banking training. All new joiners have an orientation tour of the department. In addition, when a request is placed by a banker, the researcher at the reference desk will explain to them what's available and what's not available, and what the alternatives are. If they wanted, for example, information on a private German company, we would probably go to a database like Amadeus [6] or Dun & Bradstreet [36] or OneSource [102] and print off the material, rather than going to the original filing.

How do you know when you've done a thorough search, particularly when you are looking for information beyond your usual sources?

GCS: We often have a time constraint on the work we do, so we wouldn't be able to spend three days on one request. We will probably use the sources that we've used in the past, the well-known databases, and then have an extra browse around the Internet. But at some point, we have to come to the conclusion that either we can't access the information—which doesn't mean that it doesn't exist—or we have gathered enough for the purpose of the banker's work.

VC: Quite often, if the banker puts a request in for a lot of information—market sizes, market shares, industry overviews, etc.—we will, firstly, find out how the information will be used. The data may be fundamental to advising a client on entering a market or on acquiring or divesting a company, or it may just be to add an extra slide to a presentation. Sometimes we have found a excellent piece of information but the banker is unwilling to go ahead and pay for the data; that can be very frustrating.

Do any of you use country-specific Web search engines?

KM: I recently moved over from the U.S. I was accustomed to using AltaVista [4], and I find that the U.K. version, AltaVista.co.uk, is definitely helpful in finding more country-specific information.

TSC: I would probably opt for the more general search engines. When I have tried to use a country-specific search engine, many of the sites it brings up are in the native language. I don't speak any other language myself, so I'd be wasting my time going through the search results.

What Web sources do you think are crucial for international research?

KM: In investment banking, the ones that we use the most are Web sites like the Bank for International Settlements [13], the central banks in each country, and the local stock exchanges. We sometimes use sites like FT.com [52] or the NewYorkTimes.com [97]. Those are probably the main free ones. The fee-based services we use all the time are EIU [37], Profound, Investext [135], and LexisNexis.

VC: Good search engines include Google [59] and AllTheWeb [3]. The fee-based databases that I think are essential include Profound, Dialog [33], DataStar [31], LexisNexis, Reuters

Business Briefing [115], Investext, .xls [159], specialist market research databases such as Gartner [53], Forrester [51] and Jupiter [81], databases of company accounts or prospectus databases such as Global Access [54], products for creating shareholder lists such as Thomson Financial/Carson [134], ShareWorld [119] and BlockDATA [16] for trading volumes, and credit reports from Dun & Bradstreet or Standard & Poor's [125]. All of these are crucial in our day-to-day research.

But I must say that, as experienced researchers, we are frustrated by the dumbing down that takes place as databases move from an online dial-up system to the Web. I, for one, dislike using the Web for research. Once you have learned to use a database and they take away the ability to do sophisticated searching, it's so frustrating. I still prefer dial-up online services over Web-based ones and, where we have both, I will use the dial-up version. I still use dial-up databases for more than three-quarters of my research requests.

GCS: I've come across an interesting search engine called WebHelp [152], which is a live search in the sense that you can post a question and a researcher in an office somewhere in the U.S. will pick up your question, search the Web on your behalf, and get back to you with the results of that search. The few times I've used it, they came back with sites that I had found already, but I found the concept quite interesting. A chat window opens up and you have a real-time conversation with a human being somewhere who's helping you with the research, rather than just getting results from a search engine.

TSC: In many respects, good research on the Net requires basic research skills—pick your key terms before you go online, and use Boolean operators.

What trends do you see in global research? How do you think you'll be doing research differently three or five years from now?

GCS: More and more data is being aggregated on portals. The information available on the Internet is being classified and organised for us. Sites such as Free Pint [178] allow you to search by an industry and find Web sites relevant to that industry. That is an advantage because some of the work has been done for you, but it's difficult to know which criteria have been used to select the sites, and you miss other sources that you would have come across if you had used a normal search engine. But we tend to waste a lot of time trying to browse through Web sites, portals, and directories, and I think more commercial enterprises will move toward organising it for us.

VC: I anticipate more specialised databases and search engines, and wider access to information products. I have started to use specialised databases and search engines more frequently by starting off with something like Search Engine Watch [195].

Vendors will continue to move existing dial-up databases to the Web and will make them accessible to a wider user community. I hope the vendors will take advice from information professionals and will improve on the existing search capabilities of their resources. Data from global sources will be more readily available than now, but as organisations see the value of information and the potential of new revenue streams, we may have to pay for information we currently get at no charge.

Super Searcher Power Tips

➤ We try to get as many sources as possible so we can make some comparisons and make sure that one bit of data isn't wildly different from another bit.

➤ Quite often, we start with something like the Organisation for Economic Co-operation and Development, so at least you know that the data is being collected consistently.

➤ We will often call our counterparts in the appropriate country and ask for their recommendations for an authoritative source.

➤ Good search engines include Google and AllTheWeb. The essential fee-based databases include Profound, Dialog, DataStar, LexisNexis, Reuters Business Briefing, Investext, .xls, and several other specialist sources.

➤ We are at the stage now where we can start to expect to get information on the Middle East and Eastern Europe the same ways you could on Western Europe five years ago.

Appendix
Referenced Sites and Sources

RESEARCH/INFORMATION SOURCES

1. **AIM: www.aimnow.com/searchtech**
   Japanese-language Web search engine.

2. **AllKorea: www.allkorea.co.jp**
   Japanese-language Web portal that includes links to news, business, entertainment, and travel sites.

3. **All theWeb, All the Time: www.alltheweb.com**
   Also known as FAST, one of the largest general Web search engines. Includes wireless-Web pages and MP3 files, as well as the more traditional "open Web" sites.

4. **AltaVista: www.altavista.com**
   One of the largest, general Web search engines. AltaVista also has an on-the-fly translation feature, Babelfish (see separate listing).

5. **AM Best: www.ambest.com**
   Web site for one of the major publishers of information on the U.S. and U.K. insurance industries. Site includes AM Best's ratings on insurance companies. Company also publishes periodicals and directories for the insurance industry.

6. **Amadeus: www.bvdep.com**
   One of the fee-based databases available through Bureau van Dijk (see separate listing). Contains detailed financial information on 4 million European companies.

   American Graduate School of International Management
   See Global Gateway.

7. **Archivio Collettivo Nazionale dei Periodici: www.cib.unibo.it/acnp**
   Catalog of periodicals in more than 2,300 public, academic, and corporate
   libraries throughout Italy. Searchable by publication title, subject, and library.
   Most of the search screens are available in both Italian and English.

8. **Arianna: arianna.iol.it**
   Italian Web search engine and annotated Web directory. The search
   engine allows searches limited to Italian sources as well as the rest of
   the Web.

9. **Arnold Information Technology: www.arnoldit.com**
   Stephen Arnold, principal of Arnold Information Technology, maintains a list
   of international search engines, sorted by geographic region and country, at
   www.arnoldit.com/lists/intlsearch.asp.

10. **Asian Business Watch: www.asianbusinesswatch.com**
    Web search engine focusing on current news, analysis, and research pertain-
    ing to Asian business, investment, and financial markets. The site and most of
    the material it links to are free.

11. **Asian Development Bank: www.adb.org**
    Financial institution based in the Philippines and consisting of fifty-nine
    member countries, with the mission of extending loans to encourage
    economic and social development in Asia, and to provide technical
    assistance and development policies. Web site includes economic, financial,
    and demographic reports and statistics.

12. **Bancomext: www.bancomext.com**
    Web site for the Mexican Bank for Foreign Trade, which works to promote
    Mexican exporters. Information available on the site includes investment
    opportunities, industry trends and analysis, trade and investment statistics, and
    related material. Site has content in both Spanish and English.

13. **Bank for International Settlements: www.bis.org**
    International organization that fosters cooperation among central banks and
    international financial institutions. Web site includes links to the central banks
    of 100 countries.

14. **BankScope: www.bvdep.com**
    One of the fee-based databases available through Bureau van Dijk (see sepa-
    rate listing). Contains financial information on 11,000 banks around the
    world. Also includes the full text of articles and credit ratings information on
    the banks included in the database.

15. **Beverage Marketing Corp.: www.beveragemarketing.com**
    Market research company focusing on the beverage industry. Reports can be
    purchased directly through the company's Web site, or through commercial
    online services such as Dialog.

16. **BlockDATA: www.blockdata.com**
    Database targeted to the investment and financial industry. BlockDATA tracks the trading activities of brokers and trading firms. Reports can be ordered on an as-needed basis by calling AutEX, the database producer, or by subscribing to the service.

17. **Bloomberg: www.bloomberg.com**
    A company specializing in real-time financial and investment information. Bloomberg's primary service—Bloomberg Professional—delivers news on world markets, financial data, and third-party analysis. Prices start at US$1250/month.

18. **Brint: www.brint.com**
    Business- and technology-oriented Web portal. This site focuses on e-commerce and knowledge management issues, and also has links to general business resources such as company directories, associations, news services, and related information.

19. **Bureau van Dijk: www.bvdep.com**
    Bureau van Dijk-Electronic Publishing is a leading source of online business information in Europe. Its databases focus on financial information and public and private company profiles. See separate listings for Amadeus, BankScope, and Global Researcher. Pricing options include flat-fee and prepayment of "credits" toward usage of individual modules.

20. **Business Information Service: www.t-bird.edu/bis**
    Fee-based research service at the International Business Information Centre at Thunderbird, the American Graduate School of International Management. The Web site includes pricing information and sample research projects.

21. **Business Information Sources on the Internet:**
    www.dis.strath.ac.uk/business
    A selective guide to business-related search engines and guides, directories, sources for company and financial information, news sites and discussion forums on the Web, with an emphasis on U.K.-related sources.

22. **Business Reference Suite: www.galegroup.com/welcome.html**
    This collection of databases, produced by Responsive Database Services and published by the Gale Group, includes the full text of articles from the Business & Industry, Business & Management Practices, and TableBase databases. Subscriptions start at US$9000, and are based on the number of simultaneous users.

23. **CCPIT: www.ccpit.org/engVersion/indexEn.html**
    The site for the China Council for the Promotion of International Trade and the China Chamber of International Commerce includes information on agencies that promote and facilitate trade with China, a guide to doing

business in China, demographic and statistical information, and related information.

24. **Centre for Monitoring the Indian Economy: www.cmie.com**
This organization collects statistics and data on all aspects of the economy of India. Subscriptions to the print and electronic products are based on the number of users and the format of the product purchased.

25. **Cerved: www.cerved.com**
Database of Italian company information and public records. Content is primarily in Italian; search interface is in Italian and English. Cost ranges from €.72 to €76.95.

China Chamber of International Commerce
See CCPIT.

26. *CIA World Factbook*: **www.odci.gov/cia/publications/factbook**
This annual publication provides two-page profiles of each of the world's countries, with basic information on the geography, demographics, government, economy, and infrastructure of the country. The information is available at no charge through the Web site; hard copy can be purchased for US$83.

27. **CorporateInformation.com: www.corporateinformation.com**
Web portal containing information on more than 350,000 companies and thirty industries worldwide. Allows searchers to find company profiles, analyst reports, and news by company name or ticker symbol.

28. **COSMOS: www.cosmos.com.mx**
Industry portal and company directory site that lists Mexican companies, organized in broad categories. Also includes a business-to-business component that facilitates connections between suppliers and manufacturers/retailers.

29. **Country Library: www.tradeport.org/ts/countries/index.html**
A portal containing information on countries around the world, built and maintained by the Los Angeles Area Chamber of Commerce. Each country's page includes information from the National Trade Data Bank (see separate listing) and links to other Web resources.

30. **Datamonitor: www.datamonitor.com**
Global market research firm. Its research reports can be purchased via the Web site or through commercial online services such as Dialog.

31. **DataStar: www.datastarweb.com**
One of the major commercial online services. It has a stronger European focus than some of its competitors, particularly in the area of company directories. Subscription costs vary; there is an annual subscription fee of SFr. 80.00 in Europe, no annual fee in the rest of the world; transaction-based pricing.

32. **Delphes: www.ccip.fr/die/uk/delphes.htm**
French database containing abstracts of articles on European markets, products, and companies. Available through commercial online services such as Dialog and DataStar.

33. **Dialog: www.dialog.com**
One of the major commercial online services. Wide variety of databases. Subscription costs vary; there is a one-time sign-up fee of US$295 for U.S. customers, an annual subscription fee of US$72 to US$144, plus a US$75/month minimum charge; transaction-based pricing and flat-fee accounts are available. Dialog also offers Open Access, which lets non-subscribers use the service and pay by credit card.

34. **Dictionary.com: www.dictionary.com**
Web-based English-language word look-up service that includes English translations for common words in a number of languages.

35. **Dow Jones Interactive: djinteractive.com**
One of the major commercial online services. Its focus is business and financial information, with good global coverage of news sources. Also includes a Web Center of annotated sites. Subscription costs US$69/year plus per-document charges. Transaction-based pricing and flat-fee accounts are available.

36. **Dun & Bradstreet: www.dnb.com**
D&B collects financial and credit-related information on companies around the world, and produces online databases and print directories. Some information is available through its Web site at no charge, other information can be purchased at the site. D&B financial databases are also searchable on commercial online services such as Dialog, Dow Jones Interactive, and LexisNexis.

37. **EIU (Economist Intelligence Unit): www.eiu.com**
Online information product developed by the publisher of the *Economist* magazine. EIU records include analysis and forecasts of the political, economic, and business environment in more than 180 countries. Includes *Country Risk Service*, which provides five-year political, policy, and eco-nomic forecasts for individual countries. The database is available through commercial online services and directly from the publisher.

38. **EL Net: www.elnet.co.jp**
Fee-based Japanese-language database of newspaper and journal articles.

39. **ELDIS: www.eldis.org**
Web-based database supported by the Institute of Development Studies, University of Sussex. Includes links to research documents, organizations, and Web sites pertaining to international development, social policy, and the environment.

40. **eMarketer: www.emarketer.com**
Market research firm specializing in trends and analysis of the Internet, online demographics, and e-business. Offer free email newsletters and some free reports on Web site; most reports must be purchased.

Emory University
See Key International Resources.

41. **Ernst & Young International: www.ey.com/global/gcr.nsf/International/International_Home**
International portal site maintained by the consulting firm Ernst & Young. Separate pages for individual countries include links to the full text of detailed reports prepared by E&Y.

42. **Euromonitor: www.euromonitor.com**
Global market research company that sells some of its reports on the commercial online services, on market research portal sites, and through its own site. Searchers can purchase individual sections or entire reports. Also publishes print yearbooks of statistical information. See, for example, the separate listings for *Consumer Europe, Consumer International, International Marketing Data and Statistics*, and *European Marketing Data and Statistics* in the "Books, Periodicals, Email Newsletters and Discussion Groups" section.

43. **Europages: www.europages.com**
A Web-based directory of 500,000 European companies. Can be searched by company name or browsed by industry. Listings are basic—company name, address, telephone and fax numbers, and line of business.

44. **European Central Bank: www.ecb.int**
Web site for the European Central Bank, which was established in conjunction with the EU's Monetary Union and the introduction of the euro. The site includes ECB publications and reports, and access to ECB financial databases.

45. **European Union: europa.eu.int**
The main Web site for the European Union, including information on various EU organizations, EU documents, treaties, legislation, and related material. Some publications are available at no charge; others require subscriptions or are pay-per-view. Generally viewed as a good information source, but difficult to use. See also separate listing for the Eurostat database.

46. **Eurostat: europa.eu.int/comm/eurostat**
Web site developed and maintained by the European Union's Statistical Office. Includes statistical surveys, key economic indicators, and material from EU periodicals. Some material is available at no charge, other information is fee-based.

47. **Excite: www.excite.com**
One of the large general Web search engines. Includes ability to search news

photographs, news wire stories and a subject directory. Also offers extensive personalization features.

48. **Factiva: www.factiva.com**
A joint venture of Dow Jones and Reuters, Factiva produces Dow Jones Interactive and Reuters Business Briefing (see separate listings) as well as enterprise integration tools. Factiva.com is also the name of an integrated database that combines the sources from Dow Jones Interactive and Reuters Business Briefing.

FAST
See All the Web, All the Time.

49. **FedStats: www.fedstats.gov**
This U.S. federal government portal site provides links to statistics generated by the federal government as well as to federal agencies with programs dedicated to gathering and disseminating statistics.

50. **FIS Online: www.fisonline.com**
Publisher's site for the Moody's Manuals, directories with detailed information on companies, municipal utilities, and related organizations. (See also separate listing for Moodys.com.) Subscription cost is based on the resources subscribed to and the number of users.

51. **Forrester Research: www.forrester.com**
Consulting firm that produces market research reports and provides consulting services. Some of its reports and briefings are available for free to registered users; other material is available on a subscription basis.

52. **FT.com: www.ft.com**
Site developed by the *Financial Times* of London that provides access to the full text and abstracts of articles from a wide variety of sources. Unlike the major professional online services, there is no charge to view the articles.

53. **Gartner Group: www.gartner.com**
Consulting firm that produces market research reports. Particularly strong in the information technology and communications industries. Executive summaries and briefing papers are available on the company's Web site.

54. **Global Access: www.primark.com/ga**
Subscription-based database of financial information produced by Primark. This is an aggregation of information from twelve sources, including U.S. SEC filings, investment analyst reports, and articles. The focus is primarily U.S., although there is some non-U.S. coverage.

55. **Global Gateway: www.t-bird.edu/ibic/links**
Web site built and maintained by the International Business Information Centre of Thunderbird, the American Graduate School of International Management. It

includes annotated links to sources for news, world business information, country background reports, and so on.

56. **Global Market Information Database: http://212.240.205.5**
Subscription-based Web site combining several Euromonitor products, including *World Marketing Data & Statistics*, *World Marketing Forecasts*, and *Brands & Their Companies*. See also separate listing for Euromonitor.

57. **Global Researcher: www.bvdep.com**
Database produced by Bureau van Dijk (see separate listing), that contains standardized company financial information for 25,000 publicly traded companies around the world. (A subset of this database, Global Researcher-SEC, includes just U.S. companies.)

58. **Goo: www.goo.ne.jp**
Search engine and directory of Japanese sources, along with news wire stories and a shopping channel. The user interface is in Japanese.

59. **Google: www.google.com**
One of the largest Web search engines. Ranking of results is based on analysis of links to the individual sites retrieved by the search, as well as on the location and frequency of the search terms.

60. **Government Information on the Internet:
www.ifla.org/resource/primer.htm**
Web site developed by the International Federation of Library Associations and Institutions. Provides links to national governments and agencies, multinational organizations, and nongovernmental organizations, as well as to compilations of treaties and other legal documents, statistical publications, and news sources.

61. **Governments on the WWW: www.gksoft.com/govt/en**
Web-based directory of government sites and political organizations, sorted by country. Also includes sources such as *CIA World Factbook*, encyclopedias, and tourist guides.

62. **HealthSTAR: www.nlm.nih.gov/pubs/factsheets/healthstar.html**
Database of articles pertaining to health services technology, administration, and research. Consists of citations to articles, not the full text of the articles. HealthSTAR can be searched through Internet Grateful Med (igm.nlm.nih.gov) at no charge.

63. **Hong Kong Exchange: www.hkex.com.hk**
Web site for the Hong Kong stock exchange. Includes text of financial filings and press releases of listed companies as well as links to other investment-related sites.

64. **Hoover's: www.hoovers.com**
A source for public and private company profiles and industry overviews. Its

strength is in U.S. and large multinational companies, but it is expanding coverage outside the U.S., with country-specific sites for the U.K., France, Germany, Italy, and Spain. Basic company information is available for free. Individual and business subscriptions are available starting at US$200/year.

65. **IMPI: www.impi.gob.mx**
Web site of the Mexican Institute for Industrial Property, which focuses on protecting intellectual property rights, including trademarks, patents, and industrial property rights.

66. **IMR Mall: www.imrmall.com**
Aggregator of market research reports from more than forty sources. Reports can be searched and tables of contents viewed at no charge; some reports permit purchase by chapter or page as well as in their entirety.

67. **IndustryLink: www.industrylink.com**
Portal site of manufacturing and industrial companies and Web resources for vertical markets ranging from aerospace to mining and telecommunications. Also includes links to a small number of job postings, organized by industry.

68. **InfoCamere: www.infocamere.it**
Produced by a consortium of chambers of commerce in Italy, this Web site contains basic information on Italian companies, such as registration data, contact information, and financial data.

69. **Infoimprese: www.infoimprese.it**
Web directory of Italian businesses, including basic registration and descriptive information on more than five million companies. Search interface and all content is in Italian.

70. **InfoLatina: www.infolatina.com.mx**
Mexican database of full-text articles, statistics, government documents, directory information, and related material. Prices vary based on source and format.

71. **InfoNavigator: navi.ocn.ne.jp**
Japanese-language Web directory and online telephone directory, developed by NTT, the Japanese telecom company.

72. **Inter-American Development Bank: www.iadb.org**
Organization focusing on economic and social development in Latin America and the Caribbean. Web site provides access to a wide variety of trade and government financial information for the twenty-six member countries.

73. **International Business Resources on the WWW:**
globaledge.msu.edu/ibrd/ibrd.asp
An international directory maintained by the Michigan State University Center for International Business Education and Research, consisting of annotated links to global business resources on the Web.

74. **International Federation of Stock Exchanges: www.fibv.com**
    Site has a wide range of statistics of the fifty-five member stock exchanges, along with information on the various exchanges and links to related information.

75. **International Monetary Fund: www.imf.org**
    Site contains reports and working papers on topics related to global financial and economic issues, as well as country-specific reports written by IMF staff. The IMF encourages countries to use international standards in reporting economic data. See the Special Data Dissemination Standard, the General Data Dissemination System, and the Data Quality Reference sites at dsbb.imf.org.

76. **InternationalAffairs.com: www.internationalaffairs.com**
    Developed by Oxford Analytica (see separate listing), this free site includes links to news sources and major policy organizations, organized by country and topic. Also includes links to major global statistical sources.

    Investext
    See Thomson Financial Securities Data.

77. **IR Asia: www.irasia.com**
    Web site focused on investor relations information. About 2,500 companies pay to have their investor-related information hosted on the site; it includes press releases, annual reports, analyst reports, prospectuses, stock quotes, and companies' presentations to analysts.

78. **ISI Emerging Markets: www.securities.com**
    Database of full-text news, financial and economic statistics, and country and company information for emerging markets in Asia, Latin America, and Central and Eastern Europe. Flat-fee subscriptions to this database are individually negotiated.

79. **J Guide: fuji.stanford.edu/jguide**
    Web directory of Japanese information resources, developed by the Stanford University U.S.-Japan Technology Management Center. The user interface and all annotations are in English; links are often to both Japanese and English versions of Japanese sites.

80. **Japan Information Network: www.jinjapan.org**
    Extensive English-language Web site of Japanese information sources. Includes brief pages on a broad range of topics, from demographics to discussions of social changes and current trends. Also includes links to other Web resources.

81. **Jupiter Communications: www.jup.com**
    Consulting firm that produces market research reports and provides consulting services. Some reports can be purchased through the Web site; others are only available to clients.

82. **Key International Resources: www.emory.edu/LIB/CBI/IBresearch.htm**
Web site maintained by the Goizueta Business Library at Emory University. Includes links to the international business research sites recommended by the librarians, particularly for the "Global Perspectives" course.

83. **Kompass: www.kompass.com**
Global directory of about 1.5 million companies. Some information is available for free; other information is restricted to subscribers. Directory entries include brand names and detailed product classification codes as well as revenue figures and number of employees. The Kompass databases are also available through the commercial online services such as Dialog.

84. **Latin American Network Information Center: lanic.utexas.edu**
Produced by the Institute of Latin American Studies at the University of Texas at Austin. This Web site is a well-organized directory of links to information sources on Latin America.

85. **Latin American Newsletters: www.latinnews.com**
Produced by the publisher of thirteen newsletters on Latin America, the site has current news about the region and a free weekly email update.

86. **Latin World: www.latinworld.com**
Web search engine that focuses on sites and sources in Central and South America and the Caribbean.

87. **LatinFocus: www.latin-focus.com**
Focusing on Latin American economies, this site provides financial information, forecasts, analysis, and statistical data on international trade and on the economy in nine Latin American countries. Much of the information is available at no charge; some reports require payment. Prices range from US$35 to US$690.

88. **LexisNexis: www.lexisnexis.com**
One of the major commercial online services. Wide variety of databases covering business, news, and legal sources. Also allows searching of current news items on the Web. Subscription costs vary; transaction-based pricing and flat-fee accounts are available. Academic subscriptions for LexisNexis are through a somewhat limited version, called Academic Universe (www.lexisnexis.com/universe). See also separate listing for Nexis.com.

89. **Lycos: www.lycos.com**
Web search engine and directory. Lycos also has country-specific versions of its site, with the user interface in the native language. See, for example, www.lycos.it for the Italian version.

90. **MarketResearch.com: www.marketresearch.com**
This site is an aggregator of market research reports from more than 350 publishers. You can purchase the full text of reports or, in many cases, individual sections or chapters.

91. **MarkIntel: www.tfsd.com**
Aggregation of market research reports, produced by Thomson Financial Services and available through commercial online services such as Dow Jones Interactive and .xls, and directly through Thomson.

92. **MetaCrawler: www.metacrawler.com**
Web meta-search engine that executes a search across a number of Web search engines. Also offers directory of commonly searched topics.

93. **MindBranch: www.mindbranch.com**
Web site that aggregates market research reports from a number of consulting companies. Reports can be purchased through the site.

94. **Moody's: www.moodys.com**
Source for credit information, financial research, and analysis regarding corporations, banks, governments, and public debt. The Web site offers free access to basic ratings information; additional information is available to subscribers.

95. **Multex: www.multex.com**
Portal site providing access to investment analysts' reports and financial reports. Some material is free; the rest can be purchased on demand.

96. **National Trade Data Bank: www.stat-usa.gov**
Database maintained by the U.S. Department of Commerce, containing Country Commercial Guides, market research reports, and Best Market reports. It also contains U.S. import and export statistics and other statistical reports. The NTDB can be searched through Stat-USA (see separate listing) or can be purchased on CD-ROM through the National Technical Information Service (www.ntis.gov).

97. **New York Times Online: www.nytimes.com**
Web site for *The New York Times* newspaper. Requires free registration. Articles from the most current seven days are available at no charge; earlier articles (going back to 1996) are available for US$2.50 each, with discounts available for purchase of multiple articles.

98. **Nexis.com: www.nexis.com**
The news and business publications portion of LexisNexis, listed separately.

99. **Nikkei Net Interactive: www.nni.nikkei.co.jp**
Japanese business news, market data, company profiles, analyst estimates, and stock information, in Japanese and English. Single-user subscription is ¥1000/month; discounts for group subscriptions.

100. **Northern Light: www.northernlight.com**
Hybrid of one of the largest Web search engines and an extensive collection of full-text articles, market research reports, and investment analysts' reports. Searching is free; articles cost US$2.95 each, other reports vary in cost.

101. **Oanda: www.oanda.com**
Web site with currency conversion tools; historical exchange rates; and related currency, foreign exchange, and travel information.

102. **OneSource: www.onesource.com**
Commercial online service that is particularly strong in financial and business information. Includes articles, statistical and financial data, and company and industry information. Subscription costs are determined by number of users and products selected.

103. **Organisation for Economic Co-operation and Development: www.oecd.org**
The OECD is a group of thirty member countries that operates as a think tank for economic and social policy. Summaries of OECD publications, statistics, and links to other relevant resources are available on the Web site.

104. **Orientation.com: www.orientation.com**
Portal of Web-based and licensed content providing country-specific and multilingual information for business, expatriates, and travelers.

105. **Outsell: www.outsellinc.com**
Research and consulting company focused on the information content industry. The executive summaries of many reports are available at no charge; complete reports and briefings are available on a subscription basis.

106. **Overheid.nl: www.overheid.nl**
Official Dutch government Web site, containing the full text of government documents from the various ministries as well as public organizations such as schools, libraries, and healthcare institutions. Some portions of the site are in English as well as Dutch.

107. **Oxford Analytica: www.oxan.com**
Subscription-based consulting service that, among other things, provides daily news and analysis of the implications of global events for corporations, banks, international institutions, and governments. (See also separate listing for InternationalAffairs.com.)

108. **Pagine Gialle: www.paginegialle.it**
Extensive directory of Italian companies, with both browse and search features. Listings include address, phone number, and a form to contact the company directly.

109. **Perfect Information: www.perfectinfo.com**
Online document delivery company that maintains a database of company annual reports. Includes archives going back as far as fifteen years, with coverage of European, Asian/Pacific Rim, U.S., and U.K. companies. Subscription and pay-as-you-go accounts are available.

110. **PIERS: www.piers.com**
The PIERS (Port Import Export Reporting Service) database, produced by the *Journal of Commerce*, covers imports and exports passing through U.S. ports. The subscription-based database can be searched through the PIERS site directly, or through commercial online services such as Dialog.

111. **Profound: www.profound.com**
A commercial online service, specializing in providing access to individual pages of market research reports. Prices vary; most subscribers have flat-fee or enterprise-wide accounts.

112. **PROMT: www.galegroup.com**
Database produced by the Gale Group, consisting of the full text and abstracts of articles from a wide variety of business, trade, and industry press sources. PROMT can be searched through commercial online services such as DataStar, Dialog, Dow Jones Interactive, and LexisNexis, as well as directly through the publisher.

113. **Qualisteam Banking and Finance: www.qualisteam.com**
Directory with links to banking, finance, and investment resources. Users can rate the usefulness of individual sites; these scores are included in the directory.

114. **Regional development banks**
Separate regional entities established to provide loans and technical assistance in order to foster economic growth and reduce poverty. They include the Inter-American Development Bank (www.iadb.org/ENGLISH/index_english.html), the Asian Development Bank (www.adb.org), the African Development Bank Group (www.afdb.org), and the European Bank for Reconstruction and Development (www.ebrd.org).

Research Bank Web
See Thomson Financial Securities Data.

115. **Reuters Business Briefing: www.business.reuters.com**
One of the major commercial online services, containing articles from business and financial publications, market research reports, and newswire stories. Particularly strong in non-English sources. Subscriptions are based on connect-time; subscribers purchase a set number of hours of access.

116. **Sagemaker: www.sagemaker.com**
Developer of enterprise information portals. Sagemaker also licenses content from information providers and delivers breaking news directly to the desktop. Subscriptions are based on content and number of users (purchased by divine, inc.).

117. **Servizio Bibliotecario Nazionale: www.sbn.it**
Italian-language library network site covering many Italian public, academic, and corporate Italian libraries. Includes a unified online catalog of the collections of the participating libraries.

118. **Seymour-Cooke Food Research International: www.seymour-cooke.com**
Market research company specializing in the food industry. Reports can be purchased through the Web site, either in full or by the chapter.

119. **ShareWorld: www.shareworld.tfsd.com**
Database produced by Thomson Financial and accessible through the Thomson Financial Web site. Includes and analyzes shareholder information for companies around the world.

120. **SICE: www.sice.oas.org**
Web site of the Foreign Trade Information System of the Organization of American States. Contains information and documents on trade agreements and treaties within the OAS, intellectual property rights organizations, investment treaties, and related links to other Web sites. Site is in English, Spanish, French, and Portuguese.

121. **SIEM: www.siem.gob.mx**
Web site of Mexico's National Business Information Directory. Includes statistics, news, and government agency information.

122. **Singapore Exchange: www.ses.com.sg**
Web site for the Singapore stock exchange. Includes full text of financial filings and other information for listed companies.

123. **SkyMinder: www.skyminder.com**
Web-based database of full-text articles, company financial information, and company profiles. The full service requires a US$5000 deposit against which documents are charged; an abbreviated version is available on a pay-per-view basis.

124. *Il Sole 24 Ore*: **www.ilsole24ore.com**
Italian-language newspaper focusing on financial and economic news. Includes a weekly section titled "The New Economy," which looks at technology and the Internet. Also features an online archive of articles from other sources; articles cost €1-4, €155 minimum prepayment required.

125. **Standard & Poor's: www.standardpoor.com**
Produces a wide variety of financial and investment-related information, including company directories, financial credit rating services, commentary and analysis of markets and industries, and related information. Some information is available at no charge on the Web site. Some S&P databases are available on the commercial online services such as Dialog and LexisNexis.

126. **Statistical Data Locators: www.ntu.edu.sg/library/stat/statdata.htm**
Directory of links to country-specific statistical information, particularly Web sites of government and nonprofit agencies.

127. **Stat-USA: www.stat-usa.gov**
Online resource developed by the U.S. Department of Commerce; includes

international market research, trade opportunities, country profiles, and economic and financial statistics. Single-user subscriptions cost US$175; reports can also be purchased individually. See also separate listings for National Trade Data Bank and USA Trade Online.

128. **Statistics Canada: www.statcan.ca**
One-stop source for statistical information from the Canadian national statistical agency. Includes demographic, trade, and economic data. Some information is free, some involves a modest fee.

129. **STN: www.cas.org/stn.html**
Commercial online service with an emphasis on science, technology, chemical, and patent databases. An abbreviated version is available, as well as a more powerful and complex version for experienced searchers. Prices are based on connect-time and output charges.

130. **TableBase: www.galegroup.com/pdf/facts/table.pdf**
Database of tabular information dealing with companies, products, markets, and demographics extracted from published articles. TableBase is available directly from the publisher and on the commercial online services such as DataStar, Dialog, and .xls.

131. **Teikoku Databank: www.tdb.co.jp**
Japanese credit reporting company that produces several financial and corporate information databases on Japanese companies and executives. These files are available on commercial online services such as DataStar, Dialog, LexisNexis, Nikkei, and Profound.

132. **Terra: www.terra.es**
Spanish-language Web search engine and directory. The site focuses on sources from Spain and Latin America.

133. **Thomson Direct: www.thomsondirect.com**
Produced by Thomson Financial (see separate listing), Thomson Direct provides a simple Web interface to company information from a number of sources, including investment analysts' reports, financial filings, stock ownership reports, and financial news. Pricing is based on the number of users.

134. **Thomson Financial/Carson:**
www.thomson.com/Businesses/Financial.html
Database that provides information on ownership and market activity of publicly traded companies. Subscription price determined by number of users and the portions of the database needed.

135. **Thomson Financial Securities Data: www.tfsd.com**
Formerly known as Investext, this collection of investment analysts' reports can be searched through the publisher's Web site (called Research Bank Web) or through the commercial online services such as Dialog, Dow Jones Interactive, and LexisNexis.

136. **Tokyo Shoko Research: www.tsr-net.co.jp/english**
Japanese credit reporting agency that provides extensive financial and credit analyses on public and privately held companies in Japan.

137. **TradStat: www.tradstatweb.com**
Fee-based database of government trade statistics, enabling searchers to determine trade volume between any two reporting countries. Available through Dialog and DataStar.

138. **Ultimate Collection of News Links: pppp.net/links/news**
Global collection of links to electronic newspapers and other news sources, sorted by region and country.

139. **United Nations (UN): www.un.org**
This Web site provides access to UN documents, information on its agencies and member states, and a full-text search feature for UN materials. For the Food and Agriculture Organization, see www.fao.org. For the UN Economic Commission for Latin America and the Caribbean, see www.eclac.org.

140. **U.S. Agency for International Development: www.usaid.gov**
AID focuses on providing aid to countries recovering from disasters and battling poverty. The Web site includes links to country and regional profiles from various U.S. government sources, including the U.S. Department of State, the *CIA World Factbook*, and U.S. embassies. The site has write-ups of regional economic trends.

141. **U.S. Chamber of Commerce: www.uschamber.org/International**
This site includes links to country- and region-specific business councils as well as to the individual American Chambers of Commerce abroad.

142. **U.S. Department of Agriculture, Foreign Agricultural Service: www.fas.usda.gov**
The USDA's Foreign Agricultural Service Web site provides information on export marketing opportunities for U.S. food and agricultural products, statistics on food and agriculture markets, and related information.

143. **U.S. Department of Commerce, Commercial Service: www.usatrade.gov**
The U.S. Commercial Service's Web site provides global listings of trade events, international market research, and tools to help with the export process.

144. **U.S. Department of Energy: www.energy.gov**
The DoE Web site has extensive information on energy, environment, and national-security issues. It also offers free subscriptions to a wide variety of email newsletters on energy-related topics. Go to the DoE's Energy Information Administration's site (www.eia.doe.gov) for Country Analysis Briefs—overviews on each country's environment, economy, and energy-related issues.

145. **U.S. Department of State: www.state.gov**
See especially the Country Commercial Guides, prepared by the Bureau of Economic and Business Affairs, and the Country Background Notes, produced by the Bureau of Public Affairs. The department's Key Officers List, which includes postal and email addresses, phone numbers and contact names for attachés in each embassy, is at foia.state.gov/allkeypostdetails.asp.

146. **U.S. International Trade Administration: www.ita.doc.gov**
Maintained by the U.S. Department of Commerce, this site offers resources to assist U.S. companies in expanding their international business. Included are import and export statistics, advice on becoming an exporter, and information on import and export regulations, forms, and tariffs.

147. **U.S. International Trade Commission: www.usitc.gov**
Web site of the ITC, an independent agency of the U.S. government that administers U.S. trade law and provides international trade information to the government. Site includes tariff information and reports on trends in specific industries.

148. **U.S. Securities & Exchange Commission: www.sec.gov**
The SEC's EDGAR files include electronic versions of most financial reports filed with the SEC by publicly traded companies with the SEC. These can be searched at edgar.sec.gov or through third-party sites such as www.FreeEdgar.com.

149. **USA Data: www.usadata.com**
Aggregator of market research, demographic and advertising statistics, and business and residential directory listings. Clients can download mailing lists as well as industry analysis. Prices for reports range from US$15 to over US$1000.

150. **USA Trade Online: www.usatradeonline.gov**
Database of U.S. import and export information on specific commodities, produced by Stat-USA and the U.S. Census Bureau. Includes aggregated statistics, statistics broken out by country of origin or destination, and statistics broken out by specific U.S. port. Annual subscription is US$300; monthly subscription is US$50.

151. **Virgilio: www.virgilio.it**
Italian Web directory similar to Yahoo! but focused on Italian information sources.

152. **WebHelp: www.webhelp.com**
Web site that offers assistance in finding information on the Web via a real-time chat session. The basic service is free; WebHelp Express service, which promises more prompt responses, costs US$9.99/month.

153. **World Bank: www.worldbank.org**
Organization that works with developing nations to improve living standards and provide loans for development. See especially the "Data" section, which

includes national and regional statistics on topics ranging from education to macroeconomics and urban development.

154. **World Law: www.austlii.edu.au/links**
Directory of Web sites throughout the world that provide information on law-related topics. Includes official government sites, case law resources, lawyers and law firms, law libraries, and online law journals.

155. **World Reporter: www.worldreporter.net**
Database of business news from sources around the world. Most English-language articles are in full text; non-English-language sources are abstracted. Database is available through commercial online services such as Dialog, Dow Jones Interactive, and FT.com.

156. **WorldSkip: www.worldskip.com**
Source for worldwide news, information, products, and services. Includes separate portals for 220 countries with links to news sources, government agencies, travel and tourism, and cultural information.

157. **Worldwide Mergers, Acquisitions & Alliances: www.tfsd.com/products/financial**
Database of transaction information on global merger and acquisition activities. Available through the commercial online services such as Dialog, LexisNexis, and .xls, as well as directly through Thomson Financial Services Data.

158. **Xinhua News Agency: www.xinhua.org or www.xinhvanet.com/english/index.htm**
News releases from the Chinese government-sponsored news agency. Archive of releases is available on commercial online services such as DataStar, Dialog, Dow Jones Interactive, and LexisNexis.

159. **.xls: www.xls.com**
Produced by Data Downlink, this collection of business databases specializes in providing numerical information in spreadsheet format. .xls includes company directories, economic and financial data, market research, and news sources.

160. **Yahoo!: www.yahoo.com**
One of the first human-built directories (as distinct from search engines) of the Internet. Sites are organized by category and subcategory. Yahoo! also has country-specific sites, such as www.yahoo.co.jp for Yahoo! Japan and mx.yahoo.com for Yahoo! Mexico.

161. **Yupi.com: www.yupimsn.com**
Spanish-language search engine that allows searches to be limited to specific Spanish-speaking countries—primarily Latin America and Spain. Also has annotated Web directory of Latin American sources.

BOOKS, PERIODICALS, EMAIL NEWSLETTERS AND DISCUSSION GROUPS

162. ***Benn's Media*. United Business Media International Ltd.**
www.ubminfo.co.uk
Cost ranges from £162 to £339
Annual publication listing information on business and consumer newspaper, periodical, and reference book publishers; radio and TV stations; advertising agencies; and so on. Separate volumes for the U.K., Europe, and the world.

163. **BIBLIOMEX-L: www.qro.itesm.mx/~ssouto/listas/bibliomex.html**
Email discussion list for librarians in Mexico. To subscribe, send email to BIBLIOMEX-L-REQUEST@CCR.DSI.UANL.MX with the text: subscribe bibliomex-l your_first_name your_last_name

164. ***Business Information Alert*. Alert Publications, Inc.**
www.alertpub.com/hpbia.html
US$162/year for 10 issues
Newsletter for business researchers, featuring articles on research techniques and industry trends, product and book reviews, and information on industry conferences.

165. **BUSLIB-L: www.willamette.edu/~gklein/buslib.htm**
English-language business librarians' email discussion group. Very active list, with a wide variety of subscribers. To subscribe, send email to LISTSERV @LISTSERV.BOISESTATE.EDU, with the text: subscribe buslib-l your-first-name your-last-name

166. ***Charleston Advisor*. The Charleston Company. www.charlestonco.com**
US$295-$495, depending on the subscriber's organization
Quarterly publication for library professionals. Each issue has extensive reviews of information products and services as well as articles on information management and current trends.

167. ***Consumer Europe*. Euromonitor. www.euromonitor.com**
£595 for 2000/2001 edition
Reports on the market for more than 300 consumer products in sixteen European countries. Reported in both the national currency and US$, or in standard volume units (kilograms, liters, etc.). The 2000/2001 edition includes data for 1994 to 1999.

168. ***Consumer International*. Euromonitor. www.euromonitor.com**
£595 for 2000/2001 edition
Reports on the market for about 300 consumer products in twenty-seven non-European countries. Reported in both the national currency and US$, or in standard volume units (kilograms, liters, etc.). The 2000/2001 edition includes data for the period from 1994 to 1999.

169. *CyberSkeptic's Guide to Internet Research*. **BiblioData.**
www.bibliodata.com
US$159/year for 10 issues; higher price outside the U.S.
Eight-page newsletter written for the experienced Internet researcher. Each issue includes a review of a Web site, comparisons of similar Web products, discussions of search techniques and tools, and brief industry announcements.

170. *D&B Exporters' Encyclopaedia*. **Dun & Bradstreet. www.dnb.com**
US$425 for single purchase, US$570 with biweekly updates
Includes global market and export information such as shipping documentation requirements, key contacts in consulates and government offices, and trade regulations for more than 200 countries.

171. *Directory of American Firms Operating in Foreign Countries*. **Uniworld Business Publications. www.uniworldbp.com**
US$325 for print edition, US$975 for CD-ROM edition, which includes one update
Three-volume directory of 2,600 U.S. parent companies and their subsidiaries, affiliates, and branches doing business outside the U.S. Includes listing of parent companies and, by country, of the foreign locations.

172. *EContent*. **Online Inc. www.ecmag.net**
US$110/year
Monthly magazine focused on the electronic content industry, from the perspectives of the producers, aggregators, and purchasers. Emphasis is on the digital content industry itself rather than on search techniques.

173. *Encyclopedia of Global Industries*, **2nd edition, 1998. Gale Group.**
www.galegroup.com
US$420
Includes profiles of 115 global industries, including the history, development, and current status of each. Chapters are from six to twenty pages long.

174. *Europa World Year Book*. **Europa Publications.**
www.europapublications.co.uk/titles/ewyb.html
US$1450
Two-volume directory, published annually. Includes listings for international organizations, and statistics and overviews of individual countries.

175. *European Marketing Data and Statistics*. **Euromonitor International.**
www.euromonitor.com
US$450
Twenty-two years' worth of business and marketing statistical data from forty-five European countries, published every two years. The focus is on consumer and socio-economic trends.

176. *El Financiero*: **www.elfinanciero.com.mx**
US$1200/year

Mexican newspaper focusing on business, investment, and financial news. Web site includes full-text articles from the current issue. Useful source for news on Internet resources within Mexico.

177. *Find It Online: The Complete Guide to Online Research*, by Alan Schlein. **Facts on Demand Press, 2000.**
US$19.95
How to find information online, emphasizing Web-based and online resources. The focus is on business and news-related sources. Also discusses how to manage information and evaluate sources.

178. **Free Pint: www.freepint.com**
Web-based portal for information professionals. Site includes an electronic bulletin board (called the Bar), a daily update (the Tipple), and a lengthy electronic newsletter that comes out biweekly.

179. *Global Development Finance.* **World Bank. www.worldbank.org**
US$350 for CD-ROM edition, US$300 for print edition
Statistical data from more than 130 countries, reporting their public and publicly guaranteed debt. Includes time series and ten-year projections for external debt and financial flows.

180. *Informatie Professional.* **Otto Cramwinkel, Publisher. www.informatieprofessional.nl**
This monthly Dutch-language periodical features background articles on trends in the Netherlands, as well as reviews of information resources.

181. *The Information Advisor.* **Find/SVP. www.InformationAdvisor.com**
US$165/year
Monthly newsletter that focuses on reviews and evaluations of online business information sources. (The author of this book is contributing editor of *The Information Advisor.*)

182. *Information Today.* **Information Today, Inc. www.infotoday.com/it/itnew.htm**
US$62.95/year for eleven issues
Monthly tabloid targeted to the information profession. Includes late-breaking industry news as well as in-depth articles, interviews, and columns on the library and information industry.

183. *Information World Review.* **Learned Information Europe, Ltd. www.iwr.co.uk**
£45/year in the UK, £55/year elsewhere
Monthly magazine focusing on online information and the information profession. The focus is somewhat U.K.-centric, but also has good coverage of general issues pertaining to the industry.

184. *International Business Information: How to Find It, How to Use It*, 2nd edition, by Ruth Pagell and Michael Halperin. Oryx Press, 1997. www.oryxpress.com
US$84.50
This book includes chapters on sources of information pertaining to various aspects of international business research, including both hard copy and electronic resources.

185. *International Business Information on the Web: Searcher Magazine's Guide to Sites and Strategies for Global Business Research*, by Sheri Lanza. CyberAge Books, 2001. www.infotoday.com.ibidirectory.htm
US$29.95
From the publisher of *Searcher* Magazine, this is a ready-reference for anyone who uses the Internet for international business research. The book is supported by a companion Web page, and features tips, techniques, and an extensive directory of sites recommended by expert researchers.

186. *International Financial Statistics*. International Monetary Fund. www.imf.org
US$286/year
This monthly periodical, published in English, French, and Spanish, reports current financial data such as interest rates, financial liquidity, and international transactions.

187. *International Marketing Data and Statistics*. Euromonitor International. www.euromonitor.com
US$450
Twenty-two years' worth of business and marketing statistical data from non-European countries around the world, published every two years. The focus is on consumer and socio-economic trends. Subscription price includes annual Yearbook.

188. *International Media Guides*. Standard Rate & Data Service. www.srds.com
US$300 for one volume; US$1046 for all five volumes
This annual series consists of five volumes, arranged by geographic region and publication format, listing newspapers, magazines, and business publications from 200 countries.

189. *Internet News*. Tecniche Nuove. internetnews.tecnichenuove.com
60,000 lire
Italian-language monthly magazine on a wide variety of Internet-related topics. Aimed at general Internet users rather than the professional online researchers.

190. *Market Share in Japan*. Yano Research Institute. www.yano.co.jp
¥50,000 for English edition, ¥100,000 for Japanese edition
Annual reference book with market size, share, and growth statistics for

Japan's major industries. Available in English as well as Japanese. Note that the English edition covers fifty industries; the Japanese edition covers 300 industries.

191. *Monthly Panorama of European Business*. **European Union. europa.eu.int**
€162 for annual subscription
Monthly publication focusing on two manufacturing or service industry sectors in the European Union each issue; also publishes monthly statistics and commentary. Each issue is about 100 pages long.

192. *Online*. **Information Today, Inc. www.infotoday.com/online**
US$110/year
Bimonthly magazine targeted to information professionals, covering electronic information products, the Internet, and search techniques.

193. *Online Competitive Intelligence*, **by Helen Burwell. Facts on Demand Press, 1999.**
US$25.95
Information on using the Web and commercial online services to find information on competitors, industries, products, and other business-related topics.

194. *Political Risk Yearbook*. **PRS Group Inc.**
www.prsgroup.com/academic/yearbook.html
US$1200 in print or on CD-ROM, US$1495 for online version
Available to academic institutions only, this annual publication includes information on economic and political risks to business and key economic forecasts for 100 countries.

195. *Search Engine Watch*. **www.searchenginewatch.com**
This Web site offers a wide variety of information on how to use search engines and maximize Web sites for search engine indexing. An electronic newsletter is also available, along with access to subscriber-only areas of the Web site, for US$89/year.

196. *Searcher*. **Information Today, Inc. www.infotoday.com/searcher**
US$72.95/year for 10 issues; higher cost outside the U.S.
Magazine targeted to professional online researchers. Includes in-depth articles on search techniques, industry trends, and evaluations of online resources.

197. *Standard & Poor's Industry Surveys*. **Standard & Poor's.**
www.standardandpoors.com
US$10,500/year for paper subscription; also available online, with pricing based on number of users
Extensive analysis, commentary, and statistics on fifty-two major U.S. industries. Subscription includes weekly updates; each industry is updated twice annually.

198. *Super Searcher* **book series. CyberAge Books.**
     www.infotoday.com/supersearchers
     Information Today, Inc. publishes a series of Super Searcher books, each of which is a collection of interviews with researchers in a particular area of expertise. In addition to *Super Searchers Cover the World*, the series includes *Super Searchers Go to the Source, Super Searchers Do Business* (see separate listing), *Super Searchers on Mergers & Acquisitions, Super Searchers on Health & Medicine, Super Searchers in the News, Super Searchers on Wall Street, Law of the Super Searchers*, and the original two Super Searcher books, *Secrets of the Super Searchers* and *Secrets of the Super Net Searchers*.

199. *Super Searchers Do Business: The Online Secrets of Top Business Researchers*, **by Mary Ellen Bates. CyberAge Books, 1999.**
     www.infotoday.com/supersearchers
     US$24.95
     Similar in format to this book, a collection of interviews with eleven expert business researchers, primarily in the U.S.

200. *What's New in Business Information*. **Bowker Saur.**
     www.bowker-saur.co.uk
     £355/year
     Fortnightly newsletter with information on business information products and services, industry news, and reviews.

SOFTWARE UTILITIES AND TOOLS

201. **Babelfish: babelfish.altavista.com**
     Babelfish is a service of the search engine AltaVista (see separate listing) that translates text from a number of languages into English, and the reverse. User can translate a single word or phrase, or point Babelfish to a particular Web page for translation.

202. **Copernic: www.copernic.com**
     Desktop software that allows simultaneous searching of eighty search engines. Basic version is available as a free download; enhanced versions search 600 search engines and specialized sources. Cost is US$39.95 to US$79.95.

203. **FreeTranslation.com: www.freetranslation.com**
     As the name implies, this Web site offers free translation from English to six other languages, and from Spanish, French, and German to English. The site also offers fee-based automatic translation products.

204. **Inmagic: www.inmagic.com**
     Library automation and information management software used to manage

online catalogs, automatically index intranet content, and manage full-text databases.

205. **Power Translator: www.lhsl.com/powertranslator/**
Lernout & Hauspie have developed a number of translation tools, including Power Translator, a software package that translates English to and from Spanish, French, Italian, German, Portuguese, and Japanese. Cost is US$149.95.

206. **Web Translator: www.lhsl.com/powertranslator/webtranslator.asp**
Translation software developed by Lernout & Hauspie that works within Netscape Navigator or Microsoft Explorer, providing online translations on the fly. Supports Spanish, French, German, Italian, Portuguese, and Japanese to English, and English to French, German, and Spanish. Originally offered as separate product, now part of Power Translator (see separate listing).

PROFESSIONAL ASSOCIATIONS, CONFERENCES, ETC.

207. **American Marketing Association: www.ama.org**
Worldwide association of marketing professionals with active local chapters. Publishes a number of periodicals.

208. **Association of Independent Information Professionals: www.aiip.org**
An international association of approximately 700 people who either own their own information businesses or are interested in the profession. The AIIP membership directory is available at www.aiip.org/directory.asp.

209. **EBIC: www.tfpl.com/conferences/EBIC/ebic.html**
European Business Information Conference, an annual conference that focuses on the concerns of both corporate information users and information vendors.

210. **eContent Expo: www.econtent2001.com**
Two-day U.S. trade show and conference produced by Online Inc., focusing on the electronic content industry.

211. **Internet Librarian: www.infotoday.com**
Annual conference for information professionals involved in Internet research, intranet development, and content management. Produced by Information Today, Inc., publisher of the Super Searcher series.

212. **Online Information conference: www.online-information.co.uk/online**
Annual conference held in London in December. One of the largest information industry conferences in terms of attendees and number of exhibits.

213. **Sue Rugge**
Sue Rugge was a pioneer in the independent research profession, founding her first research business, Information Unlimited, in 1971. She went on to found Information on Demand and the Information Professionals Institute.

Sue wrote *The Information Broker's Handbook*—considered the definitive guide to the profession and now out of print—gave seminars on starting and running an information business, and provided advice, encouragement, and friendship to thousands of people. She passed away at the age of 58 in 1999.

214. **Society of Competitive Intelligence Professionals: www.scip.org**
An international association of competitive intelligence professionals. Members are primarily involved in corporate competitive intelligence, although some are CI consultants.

215. **Special Libraries Association: www.sla.org**
An international association of "special librarians"—primarily those in corporations, associations, and government agencies, as distinct from public or school libraries. Primarily U.S. and Canadian membership, with some non-North American regional groups as well.

216. **Web Search University: www.websearchu.com**
Regional U.S. conferences designed for experienced Web researchers, produced by Online Inc. Held twice a year.

About the Author

Mary Ellen Bates is the owner of Bates Information Services. She provides business research to business professionals and back-up research services to corporate librarians. She is also a consultant to the online information industry. Prior to starting her own business in 1992, she worked in corporate and law libraries for fifteen years. She received her Masters in Library and Information Science from the University of California, Berkeley and has been an online researcher since the late 1970s.

Mary Ellen is the author of four other books: *Mining For Gold on the Internet* (McGraw-Hill, 2000), *Researching Online For Dummies*, 2nd edition, co-authored with Reva Basch (Hungry Minds, 2000), *Super Searchers Do Business* (Information Today, 1999), and *The Online Deskbook* (Information Today, 1996). She writes the "End of File" column for *EContent* and the "Spotlight on Online" column for *ONLINE*. She is also the contributing editor of *The Information Advisor*. She is a frequent international speaker, and has given presentations at information industry conferences in the U.S., Mexico, the U.K., Denmark, Sweden, Germany, and Australia. She is a past president of the Association of Independent Information Professionals and is active in the Special Libraries Association and the Society of Competitive Intelligence Professionals.

Mary Ellen lives in Washington, DC, with her companion and her dog. She can be contacted at mbates@BatesInfo.com or www.BatesInfo.com.

Photo by David Torres

About the Editor

Reva Basch, executive editor of the Super Searcher book series, has written four books of her own: *Researching Online For Dummies* (Hungry Minds, 2nd edition with Mary Ellen Bates), *Secrets of the Super Net Searchers* (Information Today, 1996), *Secrets of the Super Searchers* (Information Today, 1993), and *Electronic Information Delivery: Evaluating Quality and Value* (Gower, 1995). She has edited and contributed chapters, introductions, and interviews to several books about the Internet and online information retrieval. She was the subject of a profile in *WIRED* magazine, which called her "the ultimate intelligent agent."

Prior to starting her own business in 1986, Reva was Vice President and Director of Research at Information on Demand, a pioneering independent research company. She has designed front-end search software for major online services; written and consulted on technical, marketing, and training issues for both online services and database producers; and published extensively in information industry journals. She has keynoted at international conferences in Australia, Scandinavia, and the United Kingdom, as well as North America.

Reva is a Past-President (1991–1992) of the Association of Independent Information Professionals and a member of the Special Libraries Association. She has a degree in English literature, *summa cum laude*, from the University of Pennsylvania, and a master's degree in Library Science from the University of California, Berkeley. She began her career as a corporate librarian, ran her own independent research business for ten years, and has been online since the mid-1970s.

Reva lives on the remote northern California coast with her husband, cats, and satellite access to the Internet.

Index